Hugo Grotius

Ætatis 62. Anno 1636

Emery Walker ph. sc.

THREE CENTURIES OF TREATIES OF PEACE

AND THEIR TEACHING

BY THE RIGHT HON.

SIR WALTER GEORGE FRANK PHILLIMORE

BART., D.C.L. LL.D.

LATE LORD JUSTICE OF APPEAL,
FORMERLY FELLOW OF ALL SOULS' COLLEGE, OXFORD

THE LAWBOOK EXCHANGE, LTD.

Clark, New Jersey

ISBN 9781584778578 (hardcover)
ISBN 9781616191054 (paperback)

Lawbook Exchange edition 2011

The quality of this reprint is equivalent to the quality of the original work.

THE LAWBOOK EXCHANGE, LTD.

33 Terminal Avenue
Clark, New Jersey 07066-1321

*Please see our website for a selection of our other publications
and fine facsimile reprints of classic works of legal history:*
www.lawbookexchange.com

Library of Congress Cataloging-in-Publication Data

Phillimore, Walter G. F. Phillimore (Walter George Frank
Phillimore), Baron, 1845-1929.
  Three centuries of treaties of peace and their teaching / Sir
Walter George Frank Phillimore.
     p. cm.
  Originally published: Boston : Little, Brown and Co., 1919.
  Includes bibliographical references and index.
  ISBN-13: 978-1-58477-857-8 (cloth : alk. paper)
  ISBN-10: 1-58477-857-1 (cloth : alk. paper)
  1. Peace treaties. 2. International law. 3. Europe--Politics and
governent. I. Title.
  KZ184.2.P45 2007
  341.6'6--dc22
                                        2007031533

Printed in the United States of America on acid-free paper

THREE CENTURIES OF TREATIES OF PEACE

AND THEIR TEACHING

BY THE RIGHT HON.

SIR WALTER GEORGE FRANK PHILLIMORE

BART., D.C.L. LL.D.

LATE LORD JUSTICE OF APPEAL,
FORMERLY FELLOW OF ALL SOULS' COLLEGE, OXFORD

BOSTON

LITTLE, BROWN AND COMPANY

1919

TO THE MEMORY OF GROTIUS

Mens provida . . .
Dissentientis conditionibus
Foedis.

UNDER WHOSE PORTRAIT
MUCH OF THIS ESSAY HAS BEEN WRITTEN

PREFACE

A PREFACE is in the nature of an apology. My excuse for the introduction of this work to the public is to be found in the following considerations:

We are all looking forward to the future peace. We are longing for it.

At the same time we are conscious how difficult it will be to make peace, how specially difficult to make a sure and lasting peace, difficult, even supposing that every nation and its rulers sincerely and heartily desire it.

Never was there a war in which so many Nations were engaged. Never has there been a settlement of so many questions as this peace will have to settle. These will not be mere questions of taking so much territory from one State and transferring it to another. The creation and dissolution of States will come under discussion. An old State may have to be divided; two old States may be thrown together. New States and Confederations may arise; old States may be submerged and destroyed.

Nor will the task be ended when the establishment and territories of the several States have been ascertained. The future peace will be a Congress of Vienna, a Hague Conference, and a Geneva Convention rolled into one. If it is to be of any value, it must not only settle the several nations of the world on a tranquil footing with a just consideration of their several claims; it must provide some securities against such another war. There must be some machinery for deterring States from embarking on war, providing other methods of determining differences, and throwing the weight of the civilised world into the scale against unlawful or wanton aggression.

And if war is to be, there must be some provisions more effectual than those we have at present, to prevent war from relapsing or degenerating into mere savagery or barbarism.

With these thoughts in my mind it occurred to me that an historical analysis of past Treaties of Peace would give some guidance for the future, that we should thereby acquire some explanation of the condition of Europe on the threshold of the present war, and see the position to which previous diplomatic settlements had brought us.

The direct origins of the present war are to be found in the Treaty which concluded the Franco-German War, in the Balkan settlement made by the Congress of Berlin, in the lasting unrest of Poland, and in the ambitions and military dominance of Germany.

None of these can be appreciated without reference to earlier times. The Franco-German

War may be looked upon either as the last stage of the remaking of Germany, or as the first achievement of the new Power.

This remaking was an ending of the constitution bequeathed by the Congress of Vienna. But what led the Congress of Vienna to frame this constitution? It was because the Emperor had lost his position as Ruler of the Empire since the Seven Years' War, and because of the position acquired by Prussia in the Treaties of Aix-la-Chapelle and Hubertsburg. Again Prussia would never have acquired this position had not the Peace of Westphalia admitted the practical independence of the several German units; while the particular rise of Prussia into the chief place among these units has to be traced back to the Treaty of Oliva and the dispossession of Sweden from the headship of the Baltic Powers.

The Balkan settlement cannot be considered apart from the state of things left by the Crimean War and the Treaty of Paris; and the Crimean War cannot be understood without reference to the previous history of wars and treaties of peace between Russia and the Porte.

Lastly, the Partition of Poland, while contributing to the aggrandisement of Austria, Russia, and Prussia, brought these three great States into over close neighbourhood, joined them for a time in a common purpose, but ended by making them jealous and fearful of each other; so that Prussia, now become Germany, could justify her vast armaments as a necessary precaution against the attack of France on one side and Russia on the other.

Notwithstanding these results, the various settlements of Europe and European Colonies by the Treaties of Peace of the last Three Centuries are not all to be condemned. Some Treaties accomplished their objects; many were useful for a time; some would have procured a long peace but for unfortunate dynastic accidents.

It seemed to me that from their success or failure some profitable lessons might be deduced; some assistance and some warnings for the future Treaty.

Then I had a second object, to see how war could be prevented and how it could be humanised and regulated if it did occur. Treaties of the eighteenth century give us lessons in regulation; treaties of the nineteenth in humanisation; while the twentieth century began with attempts at prevention, imperfect unhappily, and too weak to stand severe strain, but not without value as guides to a more perfect scheme in the future.

And so, having traced the history of the period and given a chapter to the Laws of War and their better enforcement in future, I have come in my last chapter to the suggestions to which I respectfully invite attention.

W. G. F. P.

July 26, 1917.

CONTENTS

LIST OF AUTHORITIES
TO WHICH REFERENCE IS MADE

ARIGA.
'La Guerre Sino-Japonaise.' Paris, 1896.
'La Guerre Russo-Japonaise.' 1908.

BERNARD.
'Four Lectures on Subjects connected with Diplomacy.'
By Mountague Bernard, M.A., Chichele Professor of International Law and Diplomacy, Oxford (afterwards the Right Hon. Mountague Bernard). Macmillan & Co. London, 1868.

BLUNTSCHLI.
'Le Droit International Codifié.' Par M. Bluntschli. Translated from the German by M. C. Lardy. Third Edition. Paris, 1881.

CALVO.
'Le Droit International.' Par M. Charles Calvo. Third Edition. Paris, 1880. Four volumes.

CARNEGIE ENDOWMENT FOR INTERNATIONAL PEACE.
'Signatures, Ratifications, Adhesions and Reservations to the Conventions and Declarations of the First and Second Hague Peace Conferences.' Washington, 1914.
'Nationalism and the Near East.' Oxford, 1915.

CHALMERS.
'Collection of Treaties between Great Britain and other Powers.' By George Chalmers. Stockdale. London, 1790. Two volumes.

DARBY.
'International Tribunals.' A Collection of the Various Schemes which have been propounded; and of Instances in the Nineteenth Century. By W. Evans Darby, LL.D., Secretary to the Peace Society. Fourth Edition. J. M. Dent & Co. London, 1904.

2

' ENCYCLOPÆDIA BRITANNICA.'
Titles. Greece, Poland, Prussia.

GROTIUS.
' De Jure Belli et Pacis.'

HERTSLET, SIR EDWARD.
' Map of Europe by Treaty to 1891.' Four volumes.
' Map of Africa by Treaty to end of 1908.' Second Edition.
Three volumes.

HERTSLET, LEWIS.
' Treaties and Conventions between Great Britain and
Foreign Powers so far as they relate to Commerce and
Navigation.' By Lewis Hertslet, Librarian and Keeper of
the Papers, Foreign Office. Butterworth. London, 1827.
Three volumes.

HIGGINS.
' The Hague Peace Conference.' By A. Pearce Higgins,
LL.D. Cambridge, 1909.

HOLDICH.
' Political Frontiers and Boundary Making.' By Colonel
Sir Thomas Hungerford Holdich, K.C.M.G., &c. Macmillan.
London, 1916.

HOLLAND.
' The Laws of War on Land.' By Sir Thomas Erskine Hol-
land, K.C., Chichele Professor of International Law and
Diplomacy, D.C.L., LL.D., F.B.A., &c. Oxford, 1908.

KINGLAKE.
' The Invasion of the Crimea.' By A. W. Kinglake, 1863-
1880. Six volmes.

KLÜBER.
' Droit des Gens Modernes de l'Europe.' Par J. L. Klüber.
Second Edition. Paris, 1874.

KOCH.
' Histoire abrégée des Traités de Paix entre les Puissances
de l'Europe depuis la paix de Westphalie.' Ouvrage entière-
ment refondu par F. Schoell. Brussels, 1837–1838. Four
volumes.

MARTENS, DE, AND DE CUSSY.
' Recueil de Traités, Conventions, &c., 1760 to 1856.' Par
le Baron Charles de Martens et le Baron Ferdinand de
Cussy. Leipzig, 1846–1857. Seven volumes.

MARTENS, VON.
' Receuil des Principaux Traités,' 1761–1790. By George Friedrich von Martens, Göttingen, 1791 ; 1791–1794, Göttingen, 1795. Five volumes, Supplement, Göttingen, 1802. Two volumes.

' NEW EUROPE, THE.'
Two volumes.

PHILLIMORE, The Rt. Honble. Sir ROBERT JOSEPH, Bart., D.C.L.
' Commentaries on International Law.' Third Edition. Butterworth. London, 1879 to 1885. Four volumes.

ROBERTSON and BARTHOLOMEW.
' An Historical Atlas of Modern Europe.' By G. Grant Robertson and J. G. Bartholomew. Oxford University Press, 1915.

RUHLIERE, CLAUDE CARLOMAN DE.
' Histoire de l'Anarchie de Pologne et du démembrement.' 1807.

SARPI.
' Istoria del Concilio Tridentino.' By Paolo Soave (Sarpi). Mendrisio, 1855. Seven volumes.

SCHMAUSS, JOHANN JACOB.
' Corpus Juris Publici S. R. Academici.' Edition by Francken and Schumann. Leipzig, 1774.

SCHOELL.
' Histoire des Traités de Paix.' By F. Schoell, being an edition and continuation of the work of Koch, whose work only went up to 1796. See Koch.

SPRÜNER.
' Historisch-Geographischer Hand-Atlas zur Geschichte des Staaten Europás. Von Dr. Karl von Sprüner. Gotha, 1854.

STUBBS. .
' Suzerainty,' Thesis. By Dr. Charles Stubbs. Pewtress & Co. London, 1882.

UNITED STATES.
' Treaties and Conventions concluded between the United States of America and other Powers since July 4, 1776.' Washington, 1889.
' Treaties, Conventions, International Acts, Protocols and Agreements, between the United States of America and

other Powers, 1770–1909.' Compiled by William M. Malloy under resolution of the Senate. Washington, 1910.

I am indebted to the courtesy of the American Embassy in London for the opportunity of reading these books and of perusing various uncollected treaties since 1909.

WHEATON.

'Histoire des Progrès du Droit des Gens.' Fourth Edition. Leipzig, 1868–1880. Four volumes.

'Elements of International Law.' By Henry Wheaton, LL.D. Fourth English Edition, by J. Beresford Atlay. London, 1904.

THREE CENTURIES OF TREATIES OF PEACE

CHAPTER I

CONDITIONS OF A JUST, LASTING, AND EFFECTIVE TREATY OF PEACE

IT would be a sorrow's crown of sorrow if this war—a war for the horrors of which no epithet, no string of epithets, is sufficient—were to end in a transient and hollow peace, something which is little better than an armistice or at most a truce, forcing the States of the world into armed camps, with destruction instead of production for the aims of their industry and policy.

Let there be some result worthy of all the courage and endurance which stand forth as bright points of light against the darkness and gloom of these three years of misery. Let us close them with a solid and lasting peace if it be possible.

Unhappily, during the last three hundred years there have been many such attempts, some of them entire failures, few with more than transient success. Let the nations try again. And let their statesmen, as they try, not neglect the counsels to be drawn from the experiences of the past. In an article in *The New Europe*[1] it has been well said that ' at the future Congress history and philosophy must be the handmaids of diplomacy.'

We want a lasting peace. But we want a just peace. We want it because no peace but a just peace can be counted upon as lasting : but also for higher reasons. In what sense do we speak of a just peace ? Is it retributive justice or distributive justice, the *suum cuique* of the Roman jurists ?

Both it would seem.

Retribution, no doubt, there should be. It is an element not to be forgotten, and it will be a great gain if some penalty can be exacted, sufficient to act as a deterrent and to prevent powerful States from taking war in hand unadvisedly, lightly, or wantonly. But the deterrent penalty should not take the form of depriving States of population and territory without regard to the wishes of the population of the ceded territory or without due consideration of geographical limits.

It must be remembered that we are not, as in times past, dealing with monarchs as if they were proprietors who could be made to cede portions of their estates. The days of ' Patrimonial States ' are past. We are dealing with peoples and nations. They must suffer, no doubt, for the wrong-doing of their Governments ; but they should not be permanently severed from the

[1] Vol. i. p. 268.

country to which they are attached, nor put in subjection to an alien rule merely in order to punish their former country for engaging in war.

Retribution is best exacted in money, in munitions of war, in ships, or by the destruction of fortresses and war material. Perhaps also in the punishment of those who stirred up the strife. It should be something which operates upon the existing generation and does not keep open a lasting sore. The Justice which should be the principal object in the treaty is distributive justice, justice to nations, peoples, and races ; that is, the due provision for the independence and safety of every State, small or large, the grouping of peoples according to their national desires, and the freedom of oppressed races.

If there be this justice, it is an additional advantage that an element of instability is removed. If, coupled with it, there be an appropriate retributory judgment when 'the terrible litigation of States '[1] is brought to its close, a security against groundless war is provided.

Then comes in another cardinal virtue, Prudence. What will it be wise to provide and what will it be useless or mischievous to provide for the future ?

Certain maxims should be stated as the foundations of treaties :

1. The boundaries between States must be natural, as it is called, according to geography

---

[1] 'War is the terrible litigation of States.' (Sir Robert Phillimore, *Commentaries on International Law*, vol. iii. sec. 1.)

and orography. They must be well marked, strong for defence and yet not tempting to aggression. Sir Thomas Holdich in his recent work gives some useful guidance.[1]

2. If possible, no State composed of peoples desirous of living as one nation should be divided.

3. While, however, States and their rulers remain ambitious and covetous, we cannot afford to forget the doctrine of the Balance of Power, which has been in the minds of diplomatists ever since the Treaty of Westphalia—the political maxim ' that no single State ought to be suffered to become strong enough to overbear the aggregate strength of the rest or some considerable but undefinable proportion of their aggregate strength.'[2]

[An alternative to this Balance of Power is found by some writers on present topics in a League of Peace, an idea which would perhaps find more favour were it not for the unsavoury memory of the Holy Alliance of 1815, as developed by the Congress of Laybach, 1821.]

4. The provisions of the treaty should be immediately and finally operative, not imposing upon States future obligations other than those of conformity with the law of nations, and of living at peace and amity with each other.

5. There should be no laying on of burdens or duties which impair the sovereignty or independence of the State.

[1] *Political Frontiers and Boundary Making.* Macmillan, 1916.

[2] *Lectures on Diplomacy*, by Professor Mountague Bernard (1868), p. 97 ; and see Phillimore, *Commentaries on International Law.* Intervention to preserve the Balance of Power, vol. i. sec. 402.

For treaties which impose burdens (servitudes) upon States, or which impair or qualify territorial sovereignty, tend to produce irritation and war, are not likely to be durable, and have not, with certain remarkable exceptions, endured.

6. Objections may also be made to treaties establishing a protectorate or suzerainty, whether the treaty be one made between the superior and inferior State, or be a treaty made between the superior and other independent States, whereby these other States recognise the protectorate or suzerainty of the superior over the inferior.[1]

There is a peculiar and subtle form of protectorate which is especially likely to produce international complications and war. It takes the form of a treaty authorising a specific interference by one State in the internal affairs of another State, either by constituting a protectorate of people of a particular nationality, or holding a particular religious faith, or by giving a guarantee of a particular constitution, or reigning family, or of succession to the throne.

In religious matters some of the most striking examples have been the provisions for the Dissidents in Poland, and for Christians in Turkey, and as to the Jews in Roumania. In constitutional matters, the case of Poland. As to dynasties, the Pragmatic Sanction and the Hanoverian Succession in Great Britain.

Some of the same objections apply to Treaties of Guarantee.

7. Yet there are cases in which the only

---

[1] See Holdich, p. 100.

way to take security against wanton aggression is to impose some special burden or constraint upon a State, at any rate for a time, and there are cases of servitudes where the commercial or political benefit to the dominant State is so great and the injury to the servient State so small, that they may be conveniently imposed. There are instances in which Protectorates have worked well.[1]

The device of a Protectorate with a corresponding Guarantee may prove the only way of dealing with the territories of the Turkish Empire.

8. None of the treaties imposing special obligations can be, or ought to be, expected to be perpetual. The conditions under which, and the times at which, the denunciation of such a treaty can be lawfully and properly made, are matters of the gravest importance and to be considered separately.[2]

9. There are some treaties (such as the Napoleonic treaties with Austria and Prussia) which impose such constraint upon the ceding State that no reasonable politician can expect them to endure at all, or to be otherwise than a worthless 'scrap of paper' unless the precaution is taken of securing material guarantees.

These maxims apply to the substance of treaties. But historical investigation also shows the necessity of carefully considering the question of form.

It has not been unusual in past times to attempt

---

[1] As in the case of the Ionian Islands, and in Africa *passim*. But otherwise as to the Transvaal.   [2] *Vide* Chapter VIII.

to get rid of some points of controversy by merely passing them by, or by employing vague language, and thus postponing the evil day. For example, the Treaty of Münster had left it uncertain what territory had passed to France under the cession of Alsace. The Treaty of Nimeguen left this still unsettled, and Louis XIV. set up 'Chambers of Reunion' which annexed large tracts of territory. The matter was not set right till the Treaty of Ryswick. By the Treaty of Utrecht, Acadia was ceded to Great Britain according to its ancient boundaries. Great Britain considered that these included New Brunswick, and the dispute was one of the causes of the Seven Years' War. This criticism might be applied to several of the Articles in the Conventions of The Hague Conferences.

Sometimes when there has been a cession of territory or delimitation of boundaries, the treaty-maker has been insufficiently informed upon points of geography, topography, and special condition.[1] This mischief is not so likely to occur now as it was, for instance, when the greater part of North America was unsettled, and the boundaries between Great Britain and France, and, later on, the boundary between Canada and the United States had to be drawn;[2] but if there are any dealings with territory in Africa it is a danger still to be looked for and guarded against.

[1] See Holdich, chap. xi.
[2] There have been at least five treaties and two arbitrations as to this latter frontier.

Sufficient care has not always been given to the language of the treaty. Vague terms and conditional phrases have too often been introduced. The writer would, as a lawyer, say that the drafting of treaties has often been careless. The question whether the *casus foederis* has or has not arisen is far too often raised. It may be well to make the treaty for a term of years only.

There are a number of clauses which Professor Bernard, in a passage which I am about to quote, calls ' amnesty clauses.' Some of these are common form clauses; but as time goes on they have been modified and improved to meet altered conditions. With the tremendous changes which have been brought about by, or have accompanied, the present war, these will require careful overhauling, particularly in such matters as the restoration of ordinary prisoners, the dealing with prisoners or non-prisoners charged with military or common law crimes, the position of subjects of occupied territories who have had perforce to enter into relations with their conquerors during the period of occupation (as to which there are some useful provisions in the Treaty of Shimonoseki, between Japan and China), and the future rights and duties of the inhabitants of ceded territories.

And, lastly, there is the unhappy conclusion that too much is not to be expected from any treaty. The best treaties are those which merely record conquests and cessions already *de facto* made or relinquished.

The object of this essay is to consider the development of the States-system of Europe through war and peace during the last three hundred years, and especially to bring under review the Treaties of Peace which have concluded the wars of this period, with a view to seeing how far they show compliance with the maxims and principles above set forth, and how far the violation of them has produced evil results. This review is confined to Treaties of Peace. As preliminary work for this essay, other classes of treaties have been studied. But the essay would be overladen if they were to be referred to, except sometimes incidentally.

A chapter, however, has been added for treaties concerning the Laws of War. The provisions on this subject are not usually to be found in Treaties of Peace. They occur in Treaties of Commerce and Navigation, or have been passed by Congresses summoned *ad hoc*, such as those of Geneva and The Hague. But upon this occasion opportunity must be taken to insert them into the final treaty, and this for two reasons: first, to make war less inhuman; secondly, to prevent war, by taking away from some nations the temptation to rely upon their superior capacity of committing atrocious acts as an element of success in war.

It will be necessary to have a restatement of these laws, an application of old-established principles in the form of new laws to check new developments of inhumanity, just as some Articles in the Creed were framed to meet new heresies, and some scheme of sanction to ensure the enforcement of laws old and new.

The analysis of a Treaty of Peace to which none but the belligerents are parties is, according to Professor Bernard, as follows:

A Treaty of Peace, if you dissect it, commonly divides itself into several distinct parts. First, there are what diplomatists have called the 'general articles'—a declaration that peace is restored, and a clause or clauses of 'amnesty'; the latter phrase, when used in this connection, embracing, beside what we commonly understand by it, the restitution of such conquests as are not intended to be retained and of rights which the war has suspended or interrupted, and the release of prisoners on both sides. Secondly, there are the provisions judged necessary to remove the causes out of which the war arose, redress the grievances complained of, and prevent the recurrence of them. This is the one essential thing which the negotiators have to do, and the pacification is hollow and imperfect if they fail to do it cleanly and effectually. Thirdly, there is the indemnity or satisfaction exacted by the stronger belligerent for the injury sustained and for the cost of the war. Lastly, provision is made for the due execution of the foregoing stipulations. Every Treaty of Peace does not contain all of these, much less do they uniformly occur in the same order; but of one which is complete in all its parts this is the general scheme.' [1]

Thus much for a treaty of peace to which only belligerents are parties. But there are more complicated forms. For instance, peace has not unfrequently been made under the mediation of one or more neutral States, and these have often been made parties to the treaty, and sometimes guarantors of the conditions of the treaty. As in

[1] Bernard, *Four Lectures on Subjects Connected with Diplomacy.*

comparatively recent times, the Treaty of 1850 between Prussia and Denmark was stated to be concluded with the concurrence of Great Britain as mediating Power. Her plenipotentiary, as well as the plenipotentiaries of Prussia and Denmark, signed the treaty. Other instances are the Treaty of Teschen, 1779, between Maria Theresa, Empress-Queen of Hungary, and Frederick II., King of Prussia, with certain ancillary treaties, where the mediating Powers were France and Russia, who guaranteed all the conventions and stipulations; also the Treaty of Szistowe, 1791, between the Emperor and Turkey, which was declared to have been concluded under the mediation of Great Britain, France, and the States General.

Sometimes the mediation is informal, and its only indication lies in the choice of some city in the neutral State as the place of its conclusion. Thus the war between the United States and Spain was concluded by a treaty made at Paris in 1898. And the treaty which closed the recent war between Russia and Japan was made, as it was understood, under the good offices of the United States, at Portsmouth, in the State of New Hampshire.

Sometimes the settlement of peace between belligerents has been supposed to involve such important questions affecting the Balance of Power that the greater neutral nations have been allowed to intervene and the treaty has been settled at a Congress. Though the Peace of

Westphalia directly affected only the relations of the German States *inter se* and with their immediate neighbours France and Sweden,[1] no European Power was absent from the Congress, except England, Poland, Russia, and Turkey; and even so, the Kings of England and Poland and the Grand Duke of Muscovy, as Allies of one or other of the belligerent Powers, were included in the Treaty of Osnabrück.

Every European Power except Turkey was represented at the Congress of Vienna, in 1815.

The Crimean War only directly involved Russia, Turkey, Great Britain, France, and Sardinia, but Austria and Prussia were represented at the Congress, and participated in the Treaty of Paris in 1856. Great Britain, France, Austria, and Germany were all parties to the Treaty of Berlin, 1878, which closed the war between Russia and Turkey.

[1] Spain and the States General had made a separate Peace in the previous January. The city of Basel and the Swiss Cantons had been declared free and exempt from the Empire and its Courts in the previous year. This is recited in the Treaties.

CHAPTER II

LESSONS SUPPLIED BY TREATIES OF PEACE FROM
WESTPHALIA, 1648, TO THE CONGRESS OF
VIENNA, 1815

WRITERS on public law, when they discuss the
subject of treaties generally, begin with the
Treaty of Westphalia [1] of 1648, that is, the
Treaties of Münster and Osnabrück, which to-
gether form the Treaty of Westphalia, that of
Münster being the more important.

Of it, among other things, the late Sir Robert
Phillimore, the writer's father, says that it ' recognised as its foundation that the Balance of Power
was necessary for the safety of nations, and though
the equilibrium protected by it related chiefly,
if not exclusively, to the German nations of
Europe, it gave stability to many principles of
international law.' [2]

Throughout the rest of the seventeenth, and

---

[1] Koch, in his *Histoire des Traités de Paix*; Schoell, who
revised and continued the work of Koch ; Wheaton in his *Histoire
des Progrès du Droit des Gens;* Sir Robert Phillimore, *Commentaries on International Law*, vol. ii. chap. vi., and the late
Professor Mountague Bernard, in his valuable Lectures on
Diplomacy, make this treaty their starting-point.

[2] *Commentaries on International Law*, vol. ii. sec. 45.

3   13

the eighteenth century to the wars of the French Revolution, this treaty was never forgotten. It was mentioned, revived, and ratified in most European treaties of this period.

In one sense the Congress of Vienna marks the close of a period, and we may consider that the treaties after that date fall into a second division. In another sense we may trace three divisions :

From Westphalia in 1648 to the recognition of American Independence in 1783, little consideration was paid to anything except the rights and interests of sovereigns and reigning families.

The second period, from 1783 to 1859, is marked by increased recognition of the rights of States.

Since 1859, we have been in a third period, in which little regard is paid to the supposed rights and interests of individual sovereigns or reigning families, and a new principle has arisen, viz., the rights of nationalities, not necessarily races, but populations whose languages, literature, habits and customs, and—it may be—religious worship, are of one piece, and such as to distinguish them from surrounding populations.

Long ago as it is since 1648, there are lessons to be drawn from the Treaty of Westphalia, and from the Treaty of Oliva in 1660, which is, for the nations bordering on the Baltic, as important a starting-point as the Treaty of Westphalia is for Central Europe. And lessons of encouragement—but, unhappily, more often of warning—

are to be drawn from these treaties, and all the great treaties which succeeded each other with almost bewildering rapidity up to the time of the French Revolution.

Some assistance is to be got even from a consideration of the hasty patchwork treaties dictated by the Directory, or by Napoleon, to the Sovereigns and States of the Continent. But it is not my purpose to be archaic, and more help is to be got from a consideration of the settlement made by the Congress of Vienna in 1815, and from the treaties and public acts of the century which has now elapsed since that memorable date.

Let us, then, briefly run through the treaties of the earlier period.

First, the Treaty of Westphalia, 1648.

This treaty brought to a conclusion the Thirty Years' War which began, as nearly as possible, three hundred years ago. It was the first dynastic war of our period.

In 1618 the state of Europe generally was as follows :

England and Scotland had recently come under the reign of one Sovereign, James I. of England and VI. of Scotland.

France was a compact country, but she was still without Artois and French Flanders, Franche Comté, Rousillon, Alsace, and Lorraine.[1]

The Empire of Charles V. had been divided upon his abdication. His descendants held Spain,

---

[1] Sprüner's map of Europe during the Thirty Years' War gives an admirable picture.

Naples and Sicily, Sardinia, the Milanese, Rousillon, Franche Comté, and the Spanish Netherlands, and for a time, Portugal.

The descendants of his brother Ferdinand had the hereditary dominions of Austria, Upper and Lower Austria, Styria, The Tyrol, Carinthia, Carniola, and various territories scattered throughout Germany. They also held the Empire itself, and claimed to hold by hereditary right the Kingdom of Bohemia. They had besides so much of Hungary as the Turk had not despoiled them of.

Italy, so far as it was not under Spanish rule, was divided between the Papal States, Savoy and Piedmont ruled by the Count of Savoy, certain Duchies, and the Republics of Venice and Genoa ; Corsica was ruled by Genoa.

The United Provinces of Holland, Zeeland, etc., had established their independence of Spain and were styled diplomatically the States General.

Germany was subject to the Emperor and was in theory of law one nation ruled by the Emperor and its Diet. But the Electors, Dukes, Landgraves, and so forth, were great feudatory Princes asserting rights against the Emperor, and often even their independence.

Switzerland was in existence, but as a smaller and more loosely knit confederation than that which we now know.

Sweden had been in subjection to Denmark, and her southern provinces were still Danish. She had, however, Finland, and she and Poland divided between them the eastern shore of the Baltic.

Denmark and Norway formed one kingdom.

Poland, united with the Grand Duchy of Lithuania, was a great kingdom stretching from the Baltic to the Black Sea, and having Prussia Proper as a feudatory.

The kingship was, or had become, elective, the State Church was Roman Catholic, and the combination of these two factors had led to a prolonged strife with Sweden. The Poles had elected the Swedish Heir-Apparent, who had become a Roman. The Swedes would not let him succeed to the Throne of Sweden, but chose another member of the Royal Family; whereupon a War of Succession broke out only to be terminated by the Peace of Oliva in 1660.

Russia, separated by Sweden and Poland from the rest of Europe, was of little importance to the other States.

Venice held Dalmatia, the Ionian Islands, and the Morea.

The Turk had the rest of Europe, including the greater part of what is now known as the Kingdom of Hungary. But an independent Christian prince had lately arisen in Transylvania.

In the East Indies the Portuguese had extensive settlements from which the Dutch were gradually driving them.

The Dutch also had the Cape of Good Hope.

In America France had begun her settlements in Acadia and Canada.

England had made a footing in New England and in Virginia.

Mexico, Florida, Central America, and South America were subject to Spanish rule either as directly Spanish or as Portuguese.

In this state of things religious persecution, launched under the auspices of the Emperor in Bohemia, led to an insurrection at Prague in 1618, and to the Bohemians, on the death of their Emperor-King, claiming that the Throne was an elective one and choosing, instead of the new Emperor, the Elector Palatine, son-in-law of James I.

Then the war began. The Elector was soon ejected from Bohemia, and his hereditary dominions were overrun by Spanish troops from the Netherlands. The Protestant States in Germany took up the cause of the Elector, partly on religious grounds, partly because it did not suit them to have a Prince of the Empire humbled. They formed a League under the King of Denmark which was in its turn defeated. Then Gustavus Adolphus, King of Sweden, descended upon Germany from the north and carried all before him till his death at the battle of Lützen. The Swedish Army remained in Germany and the contest went on with varying success.

In the meanwhile the Spaniards had gone to war with the States General. France allied herself with the States General, sent succour to the Protestant German States, and invaded Lorraine and Alsace. Portugal revolted from Spain, and there was an insurrection in Catalonia.

At last the war was brought to a close by the exhaustion of all concerned. Negotiations began in 1645, but the Peace was not concluded till 1648.

It had the merit of settling a long and bloody war. It recognised the possession by France of Alsace (with some limitations) and of the three Bishoprics in Lorraine, a possession which lasted till the Franco-German War of 1870–71—upwards of two hundred years. It principally affected Germany, which it pacified. It did good inasmuch as it pacified, and inasmuch as it made an advance towards religious toleration ; and it made the absolute dominion of the Emperor over the whole of Germany impossible, and in that way contributed to the Balance of Power.

But its mischief was that it established a number of Princes and States in an anomalous position of quasi-independence, most of them so weak that they could not resist the encroachments of France or Sweden, and yet unwilling, through mutual jealousies, to combine for the common interests of Germany.

And a still greater evil. It gave right to France and to Sweden—and, later, to Great Britain and Russia—in their capacity of guarantors of the treaty, to interfere with the internal affairs of Germany, taking to themselves allies out of Germany against the common interests of the bulk of the country.

It was framed largely in the personal interests of sovereigns and dynasties, and, except in the matter of religious toleration, paid scant regard to the interests of the people.

It recognised the independence of the States General of the United Provinces of the Netherlands, but it sacrificed the commercial interests of the Spanish Netherlands by closing the Scheldt. This unfortunate provision,[1] dictated by commercial jealousy, was a constant source of irritation between the States General and the Sovereign of the Spanish—or, as they became later, the Austrian—Netherlands. We shall find it come under repeated discussion, and finally become a cause of conflict between the Emperor and the States General in 1785.

The Treaty of Westphalia left two Powers at war—France and Spain—and they so remained till the Treaty of the Pyrenees of 1659.

That treaty had one valuable provision. By it Spain ceded to France its possessions north of the Pyrenees, and from that time forward the boundary between France and Spain has followed the geographical line furnished by that chain, and the wisdom of compliance with the first maxim of prudence has been demonstrated.[2]

But on the other frontiers there was less certainty. Franche Comté (now the Departments of Doubs, Jura, and Haute Savoie) went back to Spain, to be restored again by the Peace of Aix-

---

[1] Le 14ᵉ article est devenu fameux ; il porte que les rivières de l'Escaut, comme aussi les canaux de Sas, Zwyn, et autres bouches de mer y aboutissantes, seront tenus clos du côté des Provinces-Unies. Cet article, qui ferma l'Escaut, a ruiné le commerce d'Anvers, et a donné matière aux différends entre l'empereur et les États généraux qui éclatèrent en 1785. (Koch, vol. i. p. 84.)   [2] *Vide supra*, p. 3.

la-Chapelle in 1668; while, as between France and the Spanish Netherlands, a series of advances and retrogressions on the part of France are to be found provided for in the Treaties of Aix-la-Chapelle, 1668; Nimeguen, 1678; Ryswick, 1679; Utrecht, 1713.

From this last date the unfortunate Spanish Netherlands were submitted to a succession of Barrier Treaties so-called, under the terms of which the principal fortresses on the French frontier were occupied by Dutch military forces and subject to Dutch military control. A condition of things which to the statesmen of the period seemed the height of political wisdom, but which left the unfortunate inhabitants in the most anomalous position, pointed to the Low Countries as the natural theatre of war— 'the cockpit of Europe,' as it has been called— and is in some degree responsible for the sufferings of Belgium in the present war.

There was another clause in the Treaty of the Pyrenees which was responsible for much bloodshed.

Louis XIV. was to marry the Infanta of Spain, and inasmuch as the throne of France descended, according to the Salic Law, to and through males only, but the throne of Spain might be occupied by a king descended from a female, there was a possibility of the same person becoming entitled, according to the constitutional laws of the two countries, to the thrones of both. But it was agreed by the treaty as beween the two nations that this should not be. It was a treaty between the two nations only, but it operated as a warning to the other nations of Europe ; and the effort of Louis XIV. to provide that one of his grandsons should sit on the throne of Spain with a possibility of his ultimately succeeding, if one sickly child died, to the throne of France, led to the Wars of the Spanish Succession, which were only concluded by the Peace of Utrecht, 1713. This was the second great dynastic contest of the period.

One may pause for a moment upon the Treaty of Utrecht. It is taken by many writers as the beginning of a second period of treaties. It was just over two hundred years old when the present war broke out.

This treaty settled the boundaries of France except in respect of Lorraine, the Duke of Lorraine being a Prince of the Empire, but as Duc de Bar, a feudatory of France, and practically dependent upon France, which already owned in Sovereignty the Enclaves made by the three Bishoprics, Metz, Toul, and Verdun. The treaty, avowedly framed to secure the Balance of Power, made it a fixed rule that the Crowns of France and Spain should never be on the same head. It was the attempt to tamper with this rule by Guizot in 1846,[1] which alienated Great Britain from the Government of Louis Philippe and, in the opinion of some writers, led to the fall of that monarch.

The Treaty of Utrecht was one of the first

---

[1] See Phillimore, *International Law*, vol. iii. secs. 537, 538.

treaties which dealt with the Colonial possessions in America—France ceding Nova Scotia (Acadia) and Newfoundland to England, but reserving Cape Breton ; this reservation being an instance of non-compliance with the first maxim and a further cause of trouble.

On the other hand, there were two infractions of the fourth and fifth maxims of prudence.[1]

Great Britain imposed upon France an obligation or servitude which impaired her sovereignty. It was a term of the treaty that the fortifications of Dunkirk should be rased and the port filled up.[2]

Louis XIV. at once began to make a new harbour at Mardick, a proceeding which was considered by Great Britain to be an act of bad faith.

It was also supposed, and apparently not without reason, that the clause as to Dunkirk itself was not being complied with. It was accordingly renewed in the Treaty of the Triple Alliance at The Hague in 1717 ; and Great Britain and the States General were authorised to send commissaries to see that the work was done. But in the Treaty of Aix-la-Chapelle, 1748, we find it provided that Dunkirk should remain fortified landwards, while seawards things should remain on the footing of the ancient treaties.

The matter comes up again in the Treaty of Paris in 1763, and it is not till the Treaty of Versailles, 1783, that Great Britain desists from

[1] *Vide supra,* p. 4.   [2] Article 9.

this requirement. By Article 17, Great Britain consented to the abrogation of all the Articles in all the former treaties concerning Dunkirk, a remarkable instance of the futility of such a clause for all purposes of good and its power as a source of trouble.

Another infraction of the same maxim was a clause concerning America, one which has had a remarkable history. France was to have the right of fishing and drying fish upon certain parts of the coast of Newfoundland, and other rights of fishery in adjacent waters.[1] This provision has been renewed as often as there has been war between France and Great Britain and peace has followed. It is renewed in the Treaty of Paris, 1763 ;[2] in the Treaty of Versailles, 1783, with some alterations as to limits ;[3] and it was again renewed at the Congress of Vienna in 1815, since which date there has happily been peace between the two countries.

It cannot be denied that the provision has led to some difficulties, and that it has not been easy in this matter for Great Britain to enforce compliance with this provision upon its colonists in Newfoundland. Very drastic action, in order to preserve the peace, was taken on one occasion by the naval officer in command—so drastic that it was ultimately held by the Judicial Committee of the Privy Council that he had exceeded his constitutional rights.[4]   But the world cannot but

---

[1] Article 13.   [2] Article 5.   [3] Articles 5 and 6.
[4] Walker *v.* Baird, *Law Reports*, 1892, Appeal Cases, p. 491.

be grateful for a provision which has created that
fine body of Breton seamen so well described in
the novels of Pierre Loti.

It is unnecessary to trouble the readers of this
essay with the details of the various Treaties of
Alliance, Counter-Alliance, and Peace which follow
in bewildering succession from the Treaty of
Utrecht to the French Revolution.

At different times Great Britain and all the
Powers of the Continent—except perhaps the
Papal States, Switzerland, and Turkey—find themselves at war with, or in alliance with, every other
Power. The permutations and combinations of
alliance or hostility afford material for a mathe-
matician. Certain principles may be deduced.
The regard paid to dynastic considerations and
extended not only to the reigning family, but to
rights in reversion of other princely families, at
the expense of national and geographical considerations, led to much bloodshed, brought about
constant shiftings of territory to the detriment of
the unhappy populations and to the great economic
loss of Europe and, one may add, of North
America. The undoing of this mischief has been
the work of the third period from 1859 to the
present day, and is still incomplete.

The territories which have been principally
submitted to this shifting process are, as already
stated, the Spanish Netherlands, the States of
Germany, the States comprised in the present
Kingdom of Italy, the lands lying round the Baltic,
and Nova Scotia (Acadia) and Cape Breton.

In Alsace the feudal rights left to German Princes over various territories in that province furnished a pretext, if not a motive, for the outbreak of war between the First Coalition and France in 1791.[1] As to Lorraine, the Duke of that country, after seeing his territory almost in constant occupation by France, or by the Emperor, finally ceded his State to Stanislas Lesczinski, who, because he was the father-in-law of Louis XV., and because he ceased to be the King of Poland, was to have the Duchy for his life, with reversion to France; while, on the other hand, the House of Lorraine was to be indemnified with the Grand Duchy of Tuscany upon the death of the reigning Duke.

Tuscany, and the Duchies of Parma and Piacenza, Modena and Lucca, and the Islands of Sicily and Sardinia, are treated as counters in the game, while the rival Powers contend over the Spanish Succession and the respective claims of claimants to the Spanish Monarchy; and, later on, over the Succession to the Empire and the Austrian possessions.

One of the most remarkable instances of the hopelessness of providing by treaty for future events is shown by the fate of the Pragmatic Sanction. By this, the Emperor Charles VI. endeavoured to provide for the succession of his eldest daughter, Maria Theresa, to all the possessions of the House of Austria, with the expectation that her husband would be elected Emperor. As far as treaties could bind States and Sovereigns, this was done

[1] Koch, vol. i. p. 519.

Koch has an interesting paragraph which will bear quotation :

Il eut grand soin de faire approuver ce règlement par les États provinciaux de tous les pays héréditaires d'Autriche ; de même que par les filles de l'empereur Joseph et par leurs époux, les électeurs de Saxe et de Bavière.[1] Il obtint successivement la garantie de sa pragmatique sanction de la plupart des puissances de l'Europe.

La première qui la donna fut le roi d'Espagne ; il la promit par l'art. 12 du traité de Vienne, du 25 avril, 1725. L'impératrice de Russie prit le même engagement par son accession à l'alliance de Vienne du 6 août, 1726 ; il fut renouvelé dans l'accession de Charles VI. à l'alliance entre la Suède et la Russie, ainsi que dans l'alliance de Copenhague, que l'empereur, la Russie et la Danemarck signèrent le 26 mai, 1732, et par laquelle la dernière puissance donna la même garantie. L'électeur de Bavière, personellement intéressé dans la succession autrichienne, avait reconnu la pragmatique sanction, par l'alliance que lui et l'électeur de Cologne avaient conclue avec l'empereur, le 1er septembre, 1726. L'électeur de Cologne avait réitéré sa garantie par l'art. 3 de son alliance avec l'empereur, du 26 août, 1731. L'engagement du roi de Prusse, contracté par le traité de Wusterhausen, du 12 octobre, 1726, paraissait annulé par la non-exécution de ce traité. Le traité de Vienne, du 19 mars, 1731, assura à Charles VI. la garantie de la Grande-Bretagne et des États-généraux. L'empire germanique avait reconnu la sanction pragmatique par un avis de 11 janvier, 1732.[2] Enfin Louis XV. avait donné la garantie la plus formelle de cet ordre de succession, par l'art. 10 de la paix de Vienne du 18 novembre, 1738.

Toutes ces garanties furent insuffisantes parce que l'empereur avait négligé les vrais moyens d'assurer sa suc-

---

[1] La renonciation de la fille ainée de Joseph Ier se trouve dans Schmauss, *C. j. g. ac.*, p. 1780 ; celle de la cadette, p. 1861.

[2] Pachner Reichsschlusse, tom. iv. p. 393, Schmauss, *C. j. publ. ac.*, p. 1400.

cession à sa fille, qui étaient des finances bien administrées, et une armée complète et exercée.[1]

Upon the death of Charles VI. Prussia invaded Silesia. The Elector of Bavaria was elected Emperor, and a League was formed against Maria Theresa, many of the guarantors of the Pragmatic Sanction becoming members of the League. This was the third great dynastic contest. When peace was concluded at Aix-la-Chapelle, Prussia had gained Silesia, and the Elector of Bavaria had kept the Imperial Crown till his death.

The Treaty of Aix-la-Chapelle, 1748, was, as Mr. Holland Rose has recently observed,[2] an inconclusive peace. It left most of the Great Powers engaged dissatisfied. It had a specially harmful effect upon our North American Colonies, who are said never to have forgotten their abandonment—as they considered it—by the Mother Country when Louisberg was retroceded to France. It was not like the Peace of Utrecht, which really did for the time settle matters, putting a check to the preponderance of the Bourbon Family.

After the Treaty of Utrecht, if Charles VI. had had a son, peace might have endured till the Declaration of Independence by the United States. Indeed, there might have been no such Declaration of Independence, for the Colonies might have had no serious cause of friction with the Mother Country. The coming difficulty of

[1] Koch, vol. i. p. 271.
[2] *The New Europe*, vol. ii. p. 130.

the Austrian Succession could not have been foreseen at the date of the Treaty of Utrecht, and it might have established a Balance of Power that would have endured indefinitely.

But the Treaty of Aix-la-Chapelle, though it concluded the third dynastic contest, left its aftermath ; for it was a peace without victory, at any rate, as far as concerned two of the combatants— France and Great Britain. Great Britain was victorious on the sea and over the seas, but France had had great successes by land.

Austria also was not so beaten by Prussia as to give up the hope of recovering Silesia. It remained, therefore, an inconclusive peace, leading shortly to the Seven Years' War.

There was one humorous thing in the Treaty of Aix-la-Chapelle. It was supposed to terminate a war which never would have arisen if the Sovereigns and States that had guaranteed the Pragmatic Sanction had kept even a part of the obligations which such a guarantee imposes. A guarantor, naturally, is one who takes some active step to ensure that which he has guaranteed. · But the question of guarantee would never have arisen if some of the guarantors had not been the active breakers of the compact. Yet, after the futility of this guarantee had been demonstrated, we find the Treaty of Aix-la-Chapelle repeating the guarantee of the Pragmatic Sanction, and adding one for the Hanoverian dynasty of Great Britain !

The next peace, that after the Seven Years'

4

War, produced treaties of a more durable nature. That of Hubertsburg, 1763, recognised the *fait accompli*, left Prussia now firmly established in Silesia, treating on equal terms with Austria, and from this time forward sharing the hegemony of Germany, a state of things which, but for the temporary Napoleonic Confederation of the Rhine, may be said to have endured till the Battle of Sadowa and the Treaty of Prague in 1866. The corresponding Treaty of Paris recognised the final conquest of Canada by Great Britain from France.[1] It was an incident of the treaty that France, under an arrangement with Spain, retired from Louisiana, and thus gave up all her possessions on the North American Continent.

The Spanish position in the eastern half of the North American Continent remained in a state of flux. Louisiana, taken over from the French to the great grief of its inhabitants—one of the worst instances of a transfer of a population as if they were cattle—was conditionally retroceded to the French Republic in 1800, and by that Republic to the United States in 1803. Florida, by the Treaty of Paris, was ceded by Spain to Great Britain and recovered by Spain in 1783. It was treated like a counter in a game. Spain ceded Florida to the United States in 1819.

On the other hand Minorca, which, for all geographical reasons and in obedience to the

---

[1] With special provisions (Article 4) for liberty to ' the new Roman Catholic subjects ' of the King of Great Britain to follow their own religious worship.

first maxim, ought never to have been severed from the other Balearic Islands, was restored to Spain and never again ceded to Great Britain.

On the whole, most of that which was settled by these treaties after the Seven Years' War has endured, some of it for a hundred years, and some to the present day.

The Treaties of Versailles of 1783 are epoch-making treaties, but as they are treaties of recognition of conquests rather than of stipulations *de futuro*, they only require a passing notice. They established the Independence of the United States, but France, which had assisted the United States, got little benefit. The *status quo* as to her colonies was preserved ; she was released by Great Britain from the obligations as to Dunkirk, and she was left with a National Debt which became a factor in the subsequent Revolution.

The other points to notice are : that Canada, the recent conquest of Great Britain, remained faithful to her, that an attempt was made to draw a boundary line across North America through unknown and unoccupied lands, with the usual results.[1] The right of fishing in British waters was conceded to the inhabitants of the United States in terms which have led to dispute and arbitration ; and there was a provision that both countries should enjoy the use of the River Mississippi[2] for navigation. This may have

[1] *Vide supra*, p. 7.

[2] ' Article 8. The navigation of the River Mississippi, from its source to the ocean, shall for ever remain free and open to the subjects of Great Britain, and the citizens of the United States.'

been the precursor of the valuable Act of the Congress of Vienna as to the free navigation of the Rhine and other rivers.

Towards the close of the eighteenth century an alteration, which has had far-reaching conse-quences, was made in the Map of Europe. It was effected by armed force, though it can hardly be said that there was any war. By a process in three stages the Kingdom of Poland was obliterated from the list of European States; these were what are known as the Three Partitions of Poland, that is, of the Kingdom of Poland with the Grand Duchy of Lithuania annexed to it.

The First Partition was made by agreement between Russia, Prussia, and Austria in 1772; the Second by Russia and Prussia in 1793; and the Third by the three States dividing the residue of Poland between them in 1795. It was not without its importance that the two latter Par-titions occurred shortly after the outbreak of the French Revolution, and just as the expansive force thereby acquired by the French nation was impelled toward foreign conquest.

Some of the results attained in the First and Second Partitions may have been in them-selves desirable. They may have made for better racial and national arrangements, and for a more natural and stable distribution of territory. These points will be further elaborated in the next chapter. But whatever may be the ad-vantages of the results obtained, the means by which they were obtained were wholly unjustifiable, and established precedents of arbitrary spoliation which in time became disastrous to two, at least, of the spoliators—Prussia and Austria.

The wars consequent on the French Revolution and the successes of the Directory and of Napoleon, produced a crop of temporary French annexations and treaties, which were rather truces than instruments with any hope of permanence, and so ephemeral that they need not be recapitulated. They had, it is true, considerable bearing upon the internal rearrangements of Germany, as they produced the secularization of ecclesiastical principalities, and the mediatization of the minor sovereigns, arrangements which were preserved at the ultimate settlement by the Congress of Vienna.

Fleeting also as these treaties were, they left their mark in Italy. The Treaty of Campo Formio, 1797, divided the territories of Venice between Austria and France. Austria got Venice itself, and for a time part of Dalmatia, and she kept this and got the rest of Dalmatia at the Congress of Vienna. It was a thoroughly unwarranted and unjust acquisition. It proved, so far as Venice and her Italian territory was concerned, a source of misery to the inhabitants, of perpetual irritation to the rest of Italy, and an important factor in the defeat of Austria by Prussia in 1866—a most effective moral against unjust aggrandisement.[1]

[1] *Vide infra*, Chapters III. and IV.

The other way in which Italy was affected was by the creation of the Kingdom of Italy, recognised by Austria at the Peace of Presburg in 1805. It was not such a Kingdom of Italy as we now know, for the Two Sicilies and other territories were excluded, but it first gave the idea that Italy might be a nation and not a ' mere geographical expression.'

There is nothing further to discuss till the defeat of Napoleon and the Treaty of Peace made at the Congress of Vienna, in 1815.

CHAPTER III

THE CONGRESS OF VIENNA AND ITS
LEGACIES

THE great settlement at the Congress of Vienna
in 1815 is the precedent which must be in the minds
of those who will frame our Peace.   From it the
most important lessons of encouragement and
of warning are to be drawn.

It concluded a period of twenty-three years of
warfare.   Napoleon I. had taken up the conquests
of the French Revolution.   He had added Holland,
Belgium, Germany to the Rhine, a large part of
Northern Italy, and the Illyrian Provinces to
France.   He held another large part of Italy as
a separate kingdom.   His brother-in-law was made
King of Naples.   He had formed the Confederation of the Rhine, in which others of his relations
were made rulers of some of the confederated
States.   This confederation included all Germany
that was not annexed to France nor left to Prussia
or Austria, both of which States were deprived
of much of their territory.   The Swiss Republic
was under his domination.   He had made his
brother King of Spain, and at one time held for
him a great part of Spain and Portugal.   His

checks had come in Spain and when he invaded Russia. He had been gradually beaten back till at last France was invaded and he abdicated in 1814. The Bourbons had been restored and Napoleon left to content himself with the Empire of Elba.

While the Congress of Vienna was sitting, he burst forth, returned to France, drove out the Bourbons and restored the Empire for a Hundred Days, till he was again beaten when leading his army to reconquer Belgium at Waterloo. France was once more occupied by the Allies, the Bourbons were again restored, and the work of the Congress proceeded to its completion.

The consequent mass of arrangements was enormous. The main Treaty of Vienna of June 9, 1815, has 121 Articles. The diplomatic instruments in connection with it fill 227 pages of Hertslet.[1]

The broad outlines of the principal matters disposed of are as follows :

1. The establishment of the German Confederation.

As already stated, the Treaty of Westphalia in 1648 had established the German Electors and Princes on a footing of independence and half-sovereignty, still subordinate to the Emperor, parts of the Empire for which the Emperor could make war or peace, and with Imperial Tribunals.

The success of Prussia under Frederic II.

---

[1] Hertslet, *Europe*, vol. i. pp. 60–286.

against Maria Theresa, Sovereign of Austria and
Hungary, had made Prussia a sharer in the
leadership of Germany. Napoleon's Confederation of the Rhine, and the abandonment by the
Emperor of his Imperial rights, had destroyed
the old Empire. But this dissolution was of
recent date, and some idea of unity had been
preserved by the Confederation of the Rhine.
Accordingly, in lieu of a German Empire the
German Confederation was established under the
dual leadership of Austria and Prussia with an
Assembly or Diet meeting at Frankfort. For
common military purposes there were to be
certain federal fortresses; and a quota of soldiers
was to be supplied by each of the federated
States.

Envoys might be accredited to, and sent
by, the Confederation, and the several States of
the Confederation guaranteed to each other the
safety of the confederated territories.

It has been the fashion to ridicule the Confederation as slow, clumsy, and ineffective, but it
saved Germany from attack, while its very defects
gave it the merit of being unaggressive.

It suffered a temporary internal convulsion
during the Revolutionary period, 1848–1851, and
it may be charged with having become a kind
of Mutual Insurance Society of Princes against
the growing dissatisfaction of their subjects,
and with being a hindrance to political development and colonial expansion. But it kept the
peace. And as far as one can see, if it had

remained neither would there have been the Franco-German War, 1870–1871, nor the present War.

The short history of the dissolution of the German Confederation is as follows :

One of the peculiarities of the League was that certain sovereigns entered into it in respect of their German possessions, but were not members of it in respect of other non-German territories.

As regards Austria, not only the separate Kingdom of Hungary and the Provinces, which have sometimes been styled the Kingdom of Slavonia, but also her Italian possessions formed no part of the Confederation. The same thing was true of her share of Poland, and of Prussia's share of Poland. The King of Holland was also Grand Duke of Luxemburg and Duke of Limburg, and the King of Hanover was also King of Great Britain. These latter were personal unions, not unions of the Crowns, and could be (as they have since been) sundered, the inheritance under Germanic law following to males only, and under Dutch and British law to make and females.

There remains the case of Denmark. The King of Denmark entered into the German Confederation as Grand Duke of Holstein. There were entities known as the Duchy of Schleswig and the Duchy of Holstein, which had frequently been united, and sometimes held by a member of the Royal Family of Denmark other than the King. But for some time the Duchies had either reverted to or become merged in the Crown, like our Duchy of Lancaster, or had been held by the King in personal union.

The peculiar position of Holstein as part of Germany, and yet subject to the Danish king, had already led to armed interference.[1] When the death of Frederick VII. brought about a disputed succession, King Christian succeeded without question to the Throne of Denmark, but the Duke of Augustenburg claimed under the Salic Law that he was the rightful heir to both Duchies.

The German Liberals had been much discontented with the rule of Denmark. Schleswig was not part of the Confederation, but a portion of it was German in race and language, while the other part was Danish. There was a feeling on the German side that the two Duchies should be kept united and, if possible, severed from Denmark. The Diet of Frankfort took up the cause of the Duke of Augustenburg, and decreed what was called a Federal Execution, that was, an occupation by the military forces of the Confederation, preserving the territory in dispute *in medio* till there had been a judicial decision.

This arrangement did not suit Austria and Prussia, and they interfered, invading not only Holstein, as to which there was some case, but

[1] By Prussia on behalf of the German Confederation. This was brought to a close by the Treaty of July 2, 1850, between Prussia in her own name and for the German Confederation on the one part, and Denmark on the other part, with Great Britain as mediating Power.

also Schleswig, which formed no part of the German Confederation.

This led to war with Denmark, the conquest of both Duchies, and their cession to Austria and Prussia. Disputes between these two countries as to the ultimate disposition of the Duchies led to attempts by Austria and Prussia to utilise the Confederation for their respective views. War broke out in 1866. Austria was defeated, and, by the Treaty of Prague, allowed the German Confederation to be dissolved, and the formation of a new North German Confederation under Prussia—Prussia, at the same time, annexing several of the German States.

The next step was for the North German Confederation to conclude Treaties of Alliance with all the South German States except Austria and the little Principality of Liechtenstein; and when Germany so constituted became involved in war with France and was on the road to victory, the South German States came into a new unity called the German Empire, that Empire which we now know.

The old Germany of the German Confederation of 1815, less the German territories of Austria, Liechtenstein, Luxemburg and Limburg, but augmented by Schleswig and the Polish provinces of Prussia, and the acquisition from France of Alsace-Lorraine, presided over by Prussia (herself far the largest State of the Empire), has become, instead of a somewhat passive organ, the most potent and aggressive instrument of war. The German Confederation lasted till it became aggressive, then its aggression brought about its dissolution.[1]

To return to the Congress of Vienna.

It established the affairs of Switzerland on a satisfactory footing. The position had been anomalous. There was the Swiss Confederation Proper, which itself included certain towns of the German Empire. There were the independent but allied Republics of Geneva, the Grison League and the Valais, and other territories in a special position.[2] These were now all associated in one Federation, and the Great Powers, who signed the Treaty at Vienna, promised ' solemnly to acknowledge and guarantee perpetual neutrality of the Helvetic Body.'[3] The Swiss Confederation, by public declaration, accepted that promise.

Further to protect Geneva, a portion of Savoy was neutralised. That is to say, it was provided that certain provinces ' shall form a part of the neutrality of Switzerland as it is recognised and guaranteed by the Powers.'

[1] It has not been thought necessary to dwell upon the various changes of territory between the German States *inter se*, which occupy Articles 15 to 52 of the Treaty of the Congress of Vienna.

Saxony lost much territory in favour of Prussia.

Prussia, having gained in other respects, made some cessions to Hanover.

Bavaria gained, and there were other minor arrangements.

[2] Neufchâtel retained a sort of subjection to Prussia till 1857.

[3] Article 3 of the Treaty of Paris of November 20, 1815, performing and extending the provisions of Article 92 of the Congress of Vienna.

Great Britain acquired in Europe Malta and Heligoland, which latter island she had taken from Denmark during the war ; and she acquired or retained a number of colonies and foreign possessions, some previously French, the others Dutch, which she had taken from the French after Holland had been seized by France.

Large as these acquisitions were, they have led to no unrest except in one case, and they have remained unquestioned. Except in the one instance, the comparatively few French and Dutch affected have seen no reason to complain, and have not complained ; and we may proudly say that the native inhabitants have been, at least, as well treated as they would have been under any other flag.

The reservation must be made as to the Cape Colony, where the Dutch element has, as we all know, not unfrequently come into conflict with English ideas of government. It may be said that it was not till the present War that the union of hearts has been finally cemented.

France had been the great conqueror and, being worsted in the end, lost all her conquests. In 1814 she was put back to the limits of 1792, with some additions on the N.E. frontier and in Savoy. After Waterloo, she was put back to her old limits, now called those of 1790 ; and, though the frontier on the north-eastern side has never been satisfactory, she has remained content within these limits except in the matter of Savoy and Nice, which she acquired in 1860 by peaceful means.

She suffered in her colonies, having to cede
Mauritius and the Seychelles Islands, Tobago [1]
and Santa Lucia to Great Britain, and her former
half of San Domingo to Spain. A great moral
against wanton aggression.

Spain gave some territory to Portugal, and
the old boundary line between the two countries
was restored and has remained to the present
day.

In all these respects the Congress of Vienna
built solidly.

There was a provision which was almost of
necessity temporary. The Ionian Islands had
formed part of the possessions of Venice; but the
Republic of Venice had been destroyed and was
not about to be revived. The fortune of war
had brought these islands into the possession
of Great Britain. There was no very obvious
means of disposing of them. Greece did not as
yet exist. To subject them to the Turk, or to the
absolutist Government of Austria, would have
been a cruelty. As an expedient (which probably
was recognised as temporary) it was decreed that
they should ' form a single, free and independent

---

[1] By the Peace of Paris, 1763, England retained all Canada,
Nova Scotia, Cape Breton, Grenada and the Grenadines, St.
Vincent, Dominica and *Tobago*.

She restored to France: Guadaloupe, Marie Galante, de
la Desirade, Martinique, *St. Lucia* and Belle Isle.

By the Treaty of Versailles, 1783, England ceded *Tobago*
and *St. Lucia*, but received Dominica, Grenada, St. Vincent,
St. Christopher, Nevis and Montserrat.

Thus Tobago and St. Lucia have passed backwards and
forwards.

State,' ' placed under the immediate and exclusive Protectorate of Great Britain.'   Austria, Russia, and Prussia renounced ' every right or particular protection,' and formally guaranteed all the dispositions of the treaty.[1]

Great Britain proved an honest trustee and an indulgent guardian, and when Greece had become firmly established as a nation under the present dynasty, and the inhabitants of the islands had manifested their desire to be united, she gave up her Protectorate and consented to the Union in 1863.[2]

So far, we have recapitulated what may be called the successes of the Congress of Vienna. We now come to its failures.   First, *Italy*.   The Kingdom of the Two Sicilies, with the Bourbon dynasty, was perhaps necessarily restored.   So were the Papal States to the Pope.   None of these territories had been included in the Napoleonic Kingdom of Italy ; and this arrangement might have endured, or, at any rate, there might have been separate kingdoms for Southern Italy and Sicily, if it had not been for the misgovernment of rulers.   But Northern Italy, which had for a time been united, was made the

[1] The actual instrument is subsequent to the Congress of Vienna, having been made at Paris on November 5, 1815.

[2] Treaty of July 18, 1863, between Great Britain, France, Russia, and Denmark.   And Treaty of November 14, 1863, between the Five Great Powers.

How far the dynasty whose position was so much augmented by this Union and by a monetary provision which Great Britain, France and Russia made by way of personal dotation to the monarch, has shown its gratitude may be a question for history.

victim of division and annexation, without any consideration for the peoples dealt with.

The Kingdom of Sardinia was restored. To it was added with scant consideration, but with some vain attempt to provide for the freedom of its citizens, the Republic of Genoa.[1]

Notwithstanding this provision the citizens of Genoa, accustomed to Republican institutions, suffered much under the absolute rule of Sardinia till the King's change of policy in 1848.

The old Grand Duchy and Duchies of Tuscany, Parma, Piacenza, Modena, Lucca, etc., were preserved as appanages for the junior branches of the Hapsburg and Bourbon Houses, upon purely dynastic considerations.

Austria retained the Milanese, and retained her ill-gotten acquisition of Venice, and the continental territories of Venice on the western side of the Adriatic, and kept or recovered the territories on the eastern side, some part of which had been taken by Napoleon.[2] The territories on the eastern side of the Adriatic, with a Slavonic population largely Italianised by Venice and the little sister Republic of Ragusa, and still retained by Austria after her cession of Venetia in 1866,

---

[1] 'Article 88. Les Génois jouiront de tous les droits et privilèges spécifiés dans l'acte intitulé, *Conditions qui doivent servir de bases à la réunion des états de Gênes à ceux de S. M. Sarde ;* et ledit acte, tel qu'il se trouve annexé à ce traité général, sera considéré comme partie intégrante de celui-ci, et aura la même force et valeur que s'il était textuellement inséré dans l'article présent.'

[2] *Vide supra*, p. 33.

5

supply one of the problems which will have to
be dealt with in the future treaty.

Italy, thus partitioned and said by Metternich
to be only a 'geographical expression,' was a
focus of unrest almost from the date of the
Congress of Vienna. Misgovernment of Naples
by the Bourbons began at once, and the Holy
Alliance had to threaten the Neapolitan people
to keep them in subjection.

In 1848 Charles Albert, King of Sardinia,
attacked the Austrian territories of the Milanese
on behalf of an Italian League.

The whole of Italy rose ; the King of Naples
had to promise a Constitution ; Rome was made
a Republic; the Dukes had to flee; and for a
time Venice shook off the Austrian yoke. But
the King of Sardinia was defeated and the *status
quo* was restored in 1849.

It was not till 1859 that Italy began to get her
unity, nor till 1866 that Venetia was added to
the rest of the kingdom ; nor till 1870 that the
last portion of the Papal States was also added.[1]

Thus this portion of the work of the Congress
of Vienna was unravelled and undone.

The next failure was as regards Norway.

Sweden had come unexpectedly to the
assistance of the Allies against Napoleon—unexpectedly, because her Ruler was a Frenchman,
and Bernadotte wanted his indemnity or satisfaction, to use Professor Bernard's phrase. He
might have had Swedish Pomerania, or at least

[1] *Vide infra,* Chapter IV.

that which still remained in 1809, restored to him. But Prussia, which had previously acquired the rest of Pomerania, wanted this also. The loss of Finland, which had been gradually acquired by Russia at different dates between 1743 and 1809 (the last being the date of the great loss of territory) had been severely felt by Sweden. But some part, at least, of Finland lay too near to St. Petersburg or Petrograd. Compensation could not be given in this quarter.

There remained Norway, which had long been as a kingdom united to the Kingdom of Denmark. Denmark had on the whole taken the side of France, and might be considered as a conquered country which must yield up something to the victors. With a disregard of national feeling which was nearly as characteristic of the Congress of Vienna as it had been of the congresses and treaties of the eighteenth century, the people of Norway were handed over to Sweden.

It might have been thought that the two countries would have formed a firm union. The peoples were both branches of the Scandinavian family, with languages not so dissimilar. Both were predominantly Lutheran in religion, though Sweden was episcopal and Norway unepiscopal.[1]

The two kingdoms might have grown together like England and Scotland. But whereas in the

---

[1] The Swedish episcopate claims, like the English, a direct succession, preserved notwithstanding the Reformation.

In Denmark and Norway there were at first no bishops, only superintendents, till Bügenhagen, himself only a priest, professed to convert the five Danish superintendents into bishops.

British case the King came from the smaller and weaker kingdom and there was no question of conquest, the Swedes claimed to have conquered Norway, and paid insufficient attention to Norwegian susceptibilities. There was no very definite grievance, but the two countries got more and more apart in sentiment, and finally fell asunder like two halves of a ripe nut, in 1905.

There is an isolated transaction with regard to Sweden which may be as well mentioned in this connection as elsewhere. One of the diplomatic instruments executed in connection with the Treaty of Paris of 1856 [1] was a Convention between Great Britain, France, and Russia, as to the non-fortification of the Åland Isles. Sweden had been neutral, but she had shown a sympathy with Great Britain and had made a treaty (November 21, 1855) binding herself not to give some assistance in Lapland to Russia. The Åland Isles from their position might be a menace to Stockholm if in the hands of Russia, to Petrograd if in the hands of Sweden. So, by a Convention made between Great Britain, France, and Russia, which was annexed to the general Treaty of Peace of 1856, Russia agreed that these islands should not be fortified and that no military or naval establishment should be made there.

This seems one of the worst forms of treaty. Sweden, the State to be benefited, was no party.

[1] *Vide infra*, Chapter V.

Great Britain and France could therefore at any time release Russia without consulting Sweden.

Again, if there were no other States likely to have naval forces in the Baltic, the Convention might be useful as protecting Sweden (the weaker State) and not seriously harming, though it was impinging upon, the Sovereignty of Russia. But when a new Baltic Power, Germany, arises, Russia is unable to use the islands as a *place d'armes* to protect the Gulf of Finland and her Baltic coasts, and the islands are left open to any sudden attack and occupation.

Whether Great Britain and France have, during the present War, released Russia from her agreement, the writer does not know. It would seem that they would have done well and wisely to release her.

The next failure of the Congress of Vienna was with regard to the Netherlands.

Upon the first revolt against Philip II. of Spain, portions of the Southern Netherlands had joined with Holland and Zeeland in insurrection. A line, however, was early drawn between the two portions, the southern part remaining Catholic and subject to the Spanish Crown, and passing later, under the Treaty of Utrecht in 1713, through the States General to Austria, with power to the States General to occupy barrier fortresses against France.

By the Treaty of Paris of May 30, 1814, it was provided (Art. 6) that Holland, placed under the Sovereignty of the House of Orange, should receive an accession of territory. By the Congress of Vienna (Art. 65) the ancient United Provinces of the Low Countries (that is what we know as the former Dutch Republic) and the former Belgian. Provinces (which by Art. 66 included the Bishopric of Liège), were to form the Kingdom of the Netherlands under the Prince of Orange-Nassau, described as being at that time Sovereign Prince of the United Provinces.

By Art. 73, the King of the Netherlands recognised as a basis of this union the eight Articles of the Convention of July 11, 1814, which were annexed to the Great Treaty. In this Convention there were a number of provisions for the protection of religious worship, for equality between the inhabitants of Belgium and Holland, for the representation of the Belgian provinces in the States General, and for their admission to all rights of commerce and navigation to the colonies. Again an attempt to give with one hand and take back with the other ; to make two States into one and yet stipulate that the Sovereign of the United State should treat his subjects in a particular manner.

The result was that the Union of Belgium and Holland endured for less time than the Union between Sweden and Norway.

The Belgians revolted in 1830. Their separation and independence were recognised by the Treaty of London of 1831, made between the Five Great Powers and Belgium. And matters as between Belgium and Holland still remaining

unsettled and war continuing, principally with
regard to the boundaries on the side of Luxemburg, a final settlement was made in 1839.

There were in 1839 two treaties : the principal
treaty being between the Five Great Powers and
the Netherlands, and the second treaty between
the Five Powers and Belgium. By Art. 1 of this
latter treaty the Five Powers declared that the
Articles hereunto annexed and forming the tenour
of the Treaty with the Netherlands ' are considered
as having the same force and validity as if they
were textually included in the present Act, and
that they are thus placed under the guarantee
of their said Majesties.'

By the principal treaty (Art. 7) ' Belgium,
within the limits specified in Arts. 1, 2, and 4,
shall form an independent and perpetually neutral
State. It shall be bound to observe such neutrality towards all other States.' These treaties
constitute the ' scrap of paper ' which the German
Chancellor would not allow to stand in the way
of a German invasion.[1]

One other matter in the principal treaty should
be referred to.

By Art. 9, the Act of the Congress of Vienna
with regard to rivers is to apply to the Scheldt.

[1] During the Franco-German War of 1870–1871, Great
Britain (Mr. Gladstone being Prime Minister and Earl Granville
Foreign Secretary) concluded a treaty with the North German
Confederation, by which if France invaded the neutrality of
Belgium Great Britain would ally herself with the Confederation
for the purpose of defending Belgium, and a similar treaty with
France in case the Confederation invaded Belgium.

The conservation of the river and the pilotage below Antwerp are to be under joint superintendence, and the Netherlands are to have the right to levy a toll for the West Scheldt. By Art. 14, the port of Antwerp shall continue to be solely a port of commerce.

A glance at the map will show that both branches of the Scheldt pass out between Dutch territories on either bank, with the result that while Holland is at peace, no ships of war and no military expedition can pass into Antwerp from the sea, or out of Antwerp.

This war may have shown both advantages and disadvantages accruing from this state of things. But if the reconstituted Belgium is not to be tied to a position of neutrality, which has done her—on this occasion, at least—so much harm, and if her statesmen think that the waters of the Western Scheldt should be common and that, for this purpose, she should have the small portions of Dutch territory which are on its southern bank, there is much to be said for Belgium's acquisition of these territories, making due compensation to Holland.

The historical case on one side and the other has been stated in Nos. 14 and 17 of vol. ii. of *The New Europe*. It is said that this strip of territory was conquered by Maurice of Nassau, from Spain. It has certainly remained for some hundred years in Dutch hands; and it was by the use of this territory that the Dutch were able to enforce their favourite provision, dictated by commercial jealousy, for the closing of Antwerp as a commercial port.[1]

The Emperor Joseph II. said, in 1784, that he would abandon all his grievances against Holland if he could get the opening of the Scheldt and the freedom of commerce with India.[2]

While Holland and Belgium were one during the French Revolutionary Period, and during the existence of the Congress Kingdom, from 1815 to 1831, the point did not arise. Since then the commercial freedom of Antwerp has been established by the already quoted Article of the Treaty of 1839. But for military purposes Antwerp has remained severed from the sea, and it seems to be a matter for important consideration whether this severance should continue.

The last failure was in Poland, and it is a failure under the effects of which we suffer most severely at this moment. Here some historical retrospect must be made.[3] In the seventeenth century the four nations who were of account on the shores of the Baltic were Denmark, Sweden, Poland, and Russia. Portions of Germany reached to the southern littoral and the Hanse towns were of importance. Prussia, so far as it existed, was a feudatory of Poland, or, for a short time, of Sweden. The Peace of Oliva of 1660, which was

---

[1] Stipulated in Article 14 of the Treaty of Westphalia, 1648.

[2] Esclavage que le traité de Münster lui avait imposé.

[3] Ruhlière, *Histoire de l'anarchie de Pologne et du démembrement* is a valuable history of the period to which it relates. The articles on Poland and Prussia in the *Encyclopædia Britannica* give an excellent general summary.

made up or followed by several bilateral treaties, forms an epoch when Denmark retired from her pride of place. The southern part of Sweden (Scania and Halland) was ceded by Denmark, and from that time Denmark lost the control of both shores of the Sound.

On the other hand, Sweden relinquished her suzerainty of Prussia.

As between Sweden and Poland, Northern Livonia went to Sweden and Southern to Poland ; Russia abandoned all Livonia. Poland also possessed Courland, and in right of the Grand Duchy of Lithuania which was annexed to Poland, even such Russian towns as Smolensk and the holy city of Kieff. The line as between Poland and Russia at that date is well shown in Robertson and Bartholomew's Historical Atlas,[1] and it is astonishing how much of Russia, as we now know it, was then in the Kingdom of Poland—all that is called White Russia, Black Russia, and Little Russia.

Russia had been even further restricted ; for earlier in the century she had lost most of the southern shore of the Gulf of Finland, but this was to Sweden. After 1660, began her recoveries from, or encroachments upon—whichever way one looks at it—Poland.

Some cessions were made by Poland in 1667,[2]

[1] And in Sprüner, *Historisch-Geographischer Hand-Atlas.*

[2] The Treaty of Andrusovo, 1667, between Poland and Russia, restored to the Tsar Smolensk and the other places which had been ceded in 1634, and also gave him Little Russia up to the Dnieper, along with the sacred city of Kieff.

and retaken afterwards. But the Treaty of Moscow in 1686 gave back to Russia the conquests so made by Poland, and all that part of Little Russia of which Russia was then in occupation, and Kieff, which was expressly recognised as part of the ancient patrimony of the Tsar. It was not till the Peace of Nystadt in 1721, that Russia got Livonia, Esthonia, Ingria, and a part of Carelia, from Sweden ; some of this a new acquisition, and some the recovery of territories once possessed by Russia and then lost.

This treaty brought Russia not only to the southern side of the Gulf of Finland, but also upon the Baltic.

After this date come what are known as the Three Partitions of Poland—1772, 1793, 1795.[1] And first, it is of importance—because of the warning which it gives against the insertion of clauses of this nature in treaties—to see the weapon which was in the hand of the Empress Catharine of Russia, that which supplied not the motive, but the pretext, more or less plausible, for her action.

In the Treaty of Oliva there were stipulations for the protection of the co-religionists of either Power in the territories of the other. Poland stipulated for the protection of Roman Catholics in North Livonia, and Sweden for the protection of those who were afterwards known as the ' Dissidents ' in Poland. Sweden, probably, was concerned for the Lutherans only ; but the Dis-

[1] *Vide supra*, p. 32.

sidents came in time to cover members of the
Orthodox Church as well.

In the Treaty of Moscow of 1686, by Art. 9,
Poland promised Russia not to molest members
of the Orthodox Church or Lutherans, and not
to try to make them Roman Catholics.

It was on an appeal by these Dissidents that
the Empress moved in 1764. In 1768, the treaty
between Russia and Poland provided that while
the King of Poland should be a Roman Catholic,
the Confederation of Dissidents should be recognised as legal, and that they should be protected
in their religious worship.

Having thus successfully interfered in the
affairs of Poland, Catharine was enabled further
to stipulate that the old Constitution of Poland
should be preserved with all its vices, reducing
the administration of the Kingdom, or Republic
as it was often called, to a state of powerlessness.
After that it was easy to find pretexts for inter-
fering, either because of the anarchy or in order
to continue the anarchy ; and the First Partition
was made.

As between Russia and Poland, it might be
fairly contended that both the First and the
Second Partitions restored to Russia what was
its own, or, at any rate, united peoples of practically the same race, and took from Poland a
subject Russian race.

There are no doubt those who will say that
the Little Russians are Ukrainians or Ruthenians,
and not closely akin to the ordinary Russian.

But they are more akin to the Russian than to the Pole, and they are of the Orthodox Church and not of the Roman Catholic Church.

But the gains of Prussia in both Partitions, and of Austria in the First Partition, were of a different nature. Austria annexed Eastern Galicia, which is said to be wholly Ruthenian and Orthodox, and which gained nothing if it lost nothing—I speak of its people—by the transfer; while there was no question that this was a dismemberment of what had always been Polish territory.

The position of Prussia was more complicated. The Elector of Brandenburg, in respect of his holding in Prussia—which was, generally speaking, that part of Prussia now called East Prussia—was at first only a vassal prince, for a time subordinate to Sweden, otherwise to Poland. He was called the Duke of Prussia at the time of the Peace of Oliva in 1660.

The Kingdom of Prussia dates from 1701, and even after that there was for a time some nominal suzerainty in the King of Poland. West Prussia, with Danzig, cutting off the Kingdom from the Mark of Brandenburg and the Prussian possessions in Pomerania and Silesia, and Ermeland, were assigned to Prussia at the First Partition. West Prussia is said to have been a thoroughly German land, having formed part of the possessions of the Teutonic Order.

So far the arrangement may be said to have been a natural one. Otherwise as to the Partitions of 1793 and 1795. They gave to Prussia purely Polish provinces—Great Poland, as it was called, in 1793, and the centre of Poland itself with its capital, Warsaw, in 1795.

This final division, which gave Courland and the main part of Lithuania to Russia, the rest of Galicia and of Lodomeria to Austria, and the provinces just mentioned to Prussia, extinguished Poland as a State.

The more patriotic and military Poles, emigrating to France, formed some of the best soldiers of Napoleon, and he rewarded them by constituting the Grand Duchy of Warsaw at the Treaty of Tilsit in 1807. The Grand Duchy was taken out of Polish Prussia.

It was in these circumstances that the Congress of Vienna had to deal with Poland. Austria was left with that part of Galicia and Lodomeria which she had gained at the First Partition; but did not keep what was called Western Galicia, which had been given to her on the Third.

Prussia was given the Province of Posen, but otherwise left as at the date of the First Partition.

Out of the rest of the Austrian and Prussian acquisitions, with some alteration of boundary round Byalistok in favour of Russia, a Kingdom of Poland with Warsaw as its capital, and a Republic of Cracow were constituted, and the Emperor of Russia was made King of Poland.

Then it was provided (Art. 1 of the Treaty of Vienna) that Russian Poland should have a distinct administration; and the Poles—whether subject to Russia, Austria, or Prussia—were to receive a representation and national status arranged according to that form of political existence which each of the governments to which they belonged should judge useful and suitable to give them.[1] The town of Cracow with its territories was declared to be in perpetuity a free city, independent and strictly neutral, under the protection of Russia, Austria, and Prussia (Art. 6). The Three Powers engaged to respect, and to procure the respect of, the neutrality of the town and territory.[2] On the other hand, the Cracovians were not to grant asylum or protection to refugees, deserters, or criminals (Art. 9).[3]

[1] *Congrès de Vienne.*
Article 1. Le duché de Varsovie, à l'exception des provinces et districts dont il a été autrement disposé dans les articles suivants, est réuni à l'empire de Russie. Il y sera lié irrévocablement par sa constitution, pour être possédé par S.M. l'empereur de toutes les Russies, ses héritiers et ses successeurs à perpétuité. S.M.I. se réserve de donner à cet état, jouissant d'une administration distincte, l'extension intérieure qu'elle jugera convenable. Elle prendra avec ses autres titres celui de czar, roi de Pologne, conformément au protocole usité et consacré pour les titres attachés à ses autres possessions.

Les Polonais, sujets respectifs de la Russie, de l'Autriche et de la Prusse, obtiendront une représentation et des institutions nationales, réglées d'après le mode d'existence politique que chacun des gouvernements auxquels ils appartiennent jugera utile et convenable de leur accorder.

[2] Article 6. La ville de Cracovie avec son territoire est déclarée à perpétuité cité libre, indépendante, et strictement neutre, sous la protection de la Russie, de l'Autriche et de la France.

[3] Article 9. Les cours de Russie, d'Autriche et de Prusse, s'engagent à respecter et à faire respecter en tout temps la neutralité de la ville libre de Cracovie et de son territoire ; aucune

These half-and-half measures, intended as some expression of the European conscience with respect to the unwarranted destruction of Poland, produced no result except to excite vain hopes and stir up fruitless insurrections.

On the outbreak of the French Revolution of 1830, and the revolt of Belgium from Holland in the same year, the Poles rose in insurrection and were defeated; and the result was that Poland was reduced to the position of an ordinary Russian province. They rose again in 1863, only to be reconquered and resubjected.

The action of Russia led to protest on the part of Great Britain and France. Excellent State Papers issued from the British Foreign Office, models of good writing and fine language, but mere words.

As to Cracow, the poor little Republic, isolated from all the world by its three powerful neighbours, was discovered, rightly or wrongly—it does not much matter—to be an asylum for the evildoers of the adjacent States; and by the Convention of Cracow of November 6, 1846, Cracow was

force armée ne pourra jamais y être introduite sous quelque prétexte que ce soit.

En revanche, il est entendu et expressément stipulé qu'il ne pourra être accordé dans la ville libre et sur le territoire de Cracovie, aucun asile ou protection a des transfuges, déserteurs, ou gens poursuivis par la loi, appartenants aux pays de l'une ou de l'autre des hautes puissances susdites, et que, sur la demande d'extradition qui pourra en être faite par les autorités compétentes, de tels individus seront arrêtés et livrés sans delai, sous bonne escorte, à la garde qui sera chargée de les recevoir à la frontière.

'restored' (that was the expression chosen) to Austria.

Great Britain and France protested, and protested in vain.

Perhaps the most dangerous legacy of the Congress of Vienna, and the one which will give most trouble when peace is finally settled, will be Poland, not necessarily the old Kingdom or Republic, or the Grand Duchy of Lithuania, but what may be called the irreducible minimum of Russian Poland with the Prussian Province of Posen and the Austrian Province of Galicia. Be it remembered that these Prussian and Austrian Provinces were recognised as outside the German Confederation of 1815, though Prussian Poland has been included, notwithstanding the continued protests of its representatives, in the German Empire as constituted in 1871.

6

CHAPTER IV

THE MAKING OF ITALY AND THE REMAKING OF GERMANY

THE legacies of the Congress of Vienna in respect of Western Europe have been traced down to the Franco-German War of 1870-71 in the chapter upon that Congress and its Legacies. But it would be well, where the matter comes in chronological order, to treat the making of Italy and remaking of Germany—being matters of the greatest importance to Europe and the world—a little more fully.

Those who guided the destinies of Sardinia had not given up the hope of an Italian, or at least a North Italian, unity, though they had to succumb to Austria in 1849.[1]

Under the advice of Cavour, the King of Sardinia entered into an alliance with France and Great Britain, who were defending Turkey in the Crimean War,[2] sent a contingent of soldiers to the Crimea, and procured some mention of the Italian question during the discussions of the Plenipotentiaries who were framing the Treaty of Paris in 1856. In 1859, Napoleon III. took

[1] *Vide supra*, p. 46.   [2] For this war, *vide infra*, Chapter V.

up arms as the ally of Sardinia against Austria; and Austria, being defeated in the Milanese, entered into the Preliminary Treaty of Villafranca, July 11, 1859, and the final Treaties of Zurich, November 10, 1859.

By the earliest of these treaties which was made between Austria and France, Lombardy was ceded to the Emperor of the French, who was to present it to the King of Sardinia; and there was a proposed Confederation of Italy under the Honorary Presidency of the Pope.

The idea of Napoleon III. at that time seems to have been that Sardinia should have the Milanese, that the administration of the Duchies and the Papal States should be reformed, and that Northern Italy should be made into a kind of Federation. But already the Dukes and Grand Duke had been ousted, and portions of the Papal Territories had risen in revolt, and by the time of the Treaty of Zurich, Garibaldi had occupied Naples and Sicily. Nevertheless, by that one of the three Treaties of Zurich [1] which was signed between Austria and France, an attempt was made to preserve the old idea of a North Italian Confederation with a reservation of the rights of the Grand Duke and Dukes, and a restoration of all the Papal States to the Pope.

But the Italian feeling was too strong; and in

---

[1] There were three treaties, the one mentioned in the text, a second between France and Sardinia relating to the cession of Lombardy, and a third between all three States, a general Treaty of Peace.

the result all that happened was that Austria saved Venetia; and the arrangements made between France and Sardinia saved the residue of the Papal States, Florence being later on constituted the capital; and so the Kingdom of Italy was established, not by any definite treaty—the only treaty being that affecting the Milanese.

This still left what was known as ' Italia Irredenta,' comprising the residue of the Papal States and at least Venetia, and, in a broader sense, further lands to the north and east.

But though the House of Savoy, by succeeding to the Throne of Italy, made large acquisitions, that dynasty lost, and in one sense it may be said that Italy lost, a portion of its territory. It must have been particularly galling to the dynasty to part with Savoy which had been the cradle of its race; and Nice was certainly Italian and the birthplace of Garibaldi, the Liberator of Southern Italy, Napoleon III., however, insisted upon being paid for his services, and in 1860 the County of Nice and the Duchy of Savoy were ceded by Sardinia to France.

This cession opened a new era. It purported, at any rate, to be effected with the goodwill of the ceded populations. How far the plebiscite then taken was a real expression of the feelings of the voters may perhaps be doubted; but homage was paid to the true principle; and after-events have shown that the two provinces have been welded in feeling with the rest of France.

Even so, their acquisition points a moral of warning. France was warned by the English Foreign Secretary, Lord Russell, who no doubt was accustomed to read lessons to Foreign Powers, that :

If Savoy should be annexed to France, it will be generally supposed that the left bank of the Rhine, and the 'natural limits,' will be the next object ; and thus the Emperor will become an object of suspicion to Europe, and kindle the hostility of which his uncle was the victim.[1]

When, at the conclusion of the Franco-German War, France had to cede ancient cherished territory, Bismarck is said to have pointed out that she had not lost more than she had gained in 1860.

When war broke out between Austria and Prussia in 1866, Italy joined as the Ally of Prussia, and recovered Venetia by the Treaty of Prague. This further rounding off of her territory was simultaneous with the first step in the remaking of Germany. When war broke out between France and the North German Confederation in 1870, the French had to withdraw their troops from Rome, the Italians entered the territory, a plebiscite was taken, and Rome, with the residue of the Papal States, was added to Italy.

This may be said to be nearly simultaneous with the welding of the North German Confederation and the States of South Germany into the German Empire. So the latter stages of the making of Italy were contemporaneous with the stages of the remaking of Germany.

[1] Phillimore, *Commentaries on International Law*, vol. i. sec. 403.

Now as to Germany. As pointed out in the past chapter, the effect of the quarrel between Austria and Prussia as to the disposal of the spoils which they had acquired from Denmark, led to the war of 1866 and the Treaty of Prague. By this treaty Austria agreed to the Dissolution of the old German Confederation, and gave her assent beforehand to all such territorial changes as Prussia saw fit to make, on the sole condition that Saxony should remain intact. Austria also ceded all her rights in the Duchies of Schleswig-Holstein, with a stipulation as to the people of North Schleswig, which will be mentioned shortly.

Prussia took possession of Hanover, the Electorate of Hesse, Nassau, and the city of Frankfort-on-the Main ; and Saxony having agreed to come into the Confederation, a North German Confederation was formed, whose southern boundary was the river Main. This river cut the Grand Duchy of Hesse, or Hesse Darmstadt, in two. Both Luxemburg and Limburg were excepted though north of the Main ; and the States left south and outside the Confederation were the residue of the Grand Duchy of Hesse, Baden, Würtemberg and Bavaria, and the little Principality of Liechtenstein, which has remained outside both the Confederation and the Empire.

Luxemburg became a disturbing element. Napoleon III. was supposed to have desired it as a sort of compensation for the gains of Prussia and the increased strength of his future neighbour. On the other hand, it was still within the *Zoll-*

verein, and the town had been one of the Federal fortresses of the old German Confederation.

This disturbing element was removed by the Treaty of London, 1867, between the Six Powers, the Netherlands and Belgium, as to the Grand Duchy of Luxemburg and the Province of Limburg.

By this treaty :

The Grand Duchy of Luxemburg . . . under the Guarantee of the Courts of the Five Powers shall henceforth form a perpetually neutral State.

It shall be bound to observe the same neutrality towards all other States.

The High Contracting Parties engage to respect the principle of neutrality stipulated by the present article.

That principle is and remains placed under the sanction of the collective guarantee of the Powers, signing Parties to the present Treaty, with the exception of Belgium which is itself a neutral State. (Art. 2.)

In the Franco-German War, France and Prussia separately declared that they would respect this neutrality, and they did so.

In the present War, Germany marched straight through, without even the courtesy of a preliminary demand.

It may be said in favour of the arrangement of 1867 that in a time of great strain (1870–1871) it preserved the neutrality of this little State, and that such a wanton series of breaches of treaty as have been perpetrated by Germany on the occasion of the present War, is not likely to recur, particularly if condign chastisement be now administered. But, on the other hand, the events of this War have shown that, if the stress be great enough, provisions as to neutrality are not observed, and that it would be far better if Luxemburg, like Belgium, was relieved of its ambiguous position, and if Luxemburg were itself either annexed to, or brought into close alliance with, some larger Power, perhaps Belgium.

Dutch Limburg was relieved of any connection with Germany and definitely annexed for all purposes to Holland. Any one who looks at the map and sees the position of this province will perhaps wonder that its neutrality has not been violated. The respect shown to it by Germany is a considerable testimony to her appreciation of Dutch neutrality.

The position of the South German States was for a time uncertain. There were suggestions that they might group themselves with Austria as a South German Confederation; and if now the Austro-Hungarian Empire should be broken up as a consequence of the War, and the German units should be found tending towards a union with other German elements, it would, if it were practicable, be very desirable for the peace of the world that the South German States should detach themselves and unite with German Austria.

In 1868 there was some movement towards a South German Confederation. The writer re-members a certain *Schützenfest* at Vienna in the summer of 1868, which was attended by South Germans from Bavaria, Würtemberg, and Baden, at which a demonstration was made towards this end.

But the statesmen had otherwise arranged, and treaties (which were for some time kept secret) of offensive and defensive alliance were made between the North German Confederation and the four Southern States. When war broke out between the North German Confederation and France in 1870, the forces of these States were placed under the supreme military command of the King of Prussia and contributed to the victory over France.

As the war continued, these States agreed to confederate with their Northern brethren; and on January 18, 1871, on the initiative of the King of Bavaria, the King of Prussia was proclaimed 'German Emperor,' not, be it observed, Roman Emperor or Emperor of Germany, thus not making claim to any continuity with the old Empire. On April 16, 1871, the German Empire was constituted, shortly to receive, at the conclusion of the war, the accretion of Alsace and part of Lorraine, and embracing, as already stated, within its limits the non-German provinces of Schleswig and Polish Prussia.

With regard to Schleswig, Austria had, with a late repentance, stipulated by Art. 5 of the Treaty of Prague that the populations of the northern districts of Schleswig should be ceded to Denmark, if by a free vote they expressed a wish to be united to her.

This is an example of an useless clause in a treaty. Every pact made between *A* and *B* for the benefit of *C* is of little or no advantage unless it ultimately suits one of the contracting parties to assert the rights of the third ; if it does not, the clause is of no value to *C*, though it may, in some instances, hamper *A* or *B*.[1]

The Franco-German War of 1870–71 and the cessions stipulated in favour of Germany by the Treaty of Peace in 1871, are the direct causes of the present War.   The cession of the whole of Alsace and of a good part of Lorraine took away from France a people who—though some of them were German in speech—were as entirely French in sentiment as any part of the nation.[2]   Bismarck is supposed to have deprecated a demand of this magnitude.

The lesson to be drawn is that, at any rate in modern times, when the unity of a State is so closely knit, and national sentiment is so thoroughly developed, the tearing away of a limb from the trunk makes a wound which hardly ever heals.

The *guerre de revanche* has been in the minds of all Frenchmen for a generation ; and, coupled with this was the not unwarranted fear that whenever France showed signs of strength, Germany might fall upon her and crush her.   It became almost a political necessity to make the alliance with Russia and the *Entente* with Great Britain ; and

---

[1] An example of this has been mentioned in the last chapter, the case of the non-fortification of the Åland Islands.   Prussia found means to evade the operation of the stipulation in the Treaty of Prague, and in 1879 it was formally abrogated by a treaty between the Two Powers.

[2] The novels of Erckmann-Chatrian, which used to delight our youth, afford striking indications of this.

hence the introduction of France, Belgium, and Great Britain into the present War.

> O impotence of man's frail mind
> To fate and to the future blind.
> Presumptuous and o'erweening still
> When fortune follows at its will!
> Full soon shall Turnus wish in vain
> That life untouched, those spoils unta'en.[1]

If the rectification of frontiers so as to give to Germany good strategic positions and railway lines with as much cession of territory as would be required for this purpose, had been the limit of German demands, probably the soreness of defeat would have soon been forgotten, and we should have had none of the enormous scale of armament and military establishment which for years made Central Europe into armed camps, and not unnaturally developed into the present War.

The other provisions of the Peace were simple and may be shortly enumerated. By the preliminary Treaty of Versailles, February 26, 1871, favourable consideration was stipulated for the unfortunate natives of the ceded territories, and in the final Treaty of Frankfort, May 10, 1871,

---

[1] Virgil, *Æneid*, Book IX. Conington's Translation. The original Latin—

Turno tempus erit magno quum optaverit emptum
Intactum Pallanta et quum spolia ista diemque Oderit

was the motto of Sir Robert Phillimore's pamphlet on the seizure of the Southern Envoys from the British ship *Trent* during the War of Secession. Fortunately in that case Pallas was in a state of suspended animation and good counsels permitted his restoration.

this was elaborated into Art. 2, which may form a useful precedent.

ART. 2. French subjects—natives of the ceded territories actually domiciled on that territory who shall preserve
their nationality shall up to the 1st of October, 1872, and
on their making previous declaration to that effect to the
competent authority, be allowed to change their domicile
into France and to remain there, that right in no wise impinging on the laws of Military Service in which case the
title of French citizen shall be maintained.

They shall be at liberty to preserve their immoveables
situated in the territory united to Germany.

No inhabitant of the ceded territory shall be prosecuted,
annoyed, or sought for, either in his person or his property,
on account of his Political or Military Acts previous to the
war.

Besides this, there were provisions for a large pecuniary indemnity to be secured by the military occupation of portions of the territory of France, the occupation being gradually reduced in area as each instalment of the indemnity was paid. The vexed question whether previous treaties are abrogated or not by war was solved by a special stipulation (Art. 11) that Treaties of Navigation, and a previous Convention as to International Service of Railways, and another as to Copyright should be renewed.

This is the last Treaty of Peace for Western Europe.

CHAPTER V

THE next important treaties concern Eastern Europe, and as to them there must be some retrospect.

When the Christian Powers began to enter into treaties with Turkey they procured the insertion of provisions, usually known as Capitulations, giving special protection to their subjects when trading to, or residing in, the Turkish dominions, and securing a special status for their Consuls, with an extra-territorial jurisdiction in civil and even criminal matters over the subjects of their nations.[1]

France had Capitulations going back to 1604. But those in force at the time with which we are dealing were the Capitulations of 1740, which gave to her subjects, in addition to other privileges, the right to visit the Holy Places at Jerusalem.[2]

---

[1] Phillimore, *Commentaries on International Law*, vol. i. sec. 413 ; vol. ii. part vii. chap. v.

For the English Capitulations of 1675, see *Collection of Treaties, &c., on Commerce and Navigation*, by Lewis Hertslet, 1827, vol. ii. p. 346.

[2] Phillimore, vol. i. sec. 413.

Besides these Capitulations, as the wave of Turkish Conquest over the Provinces of Hungary, Poland, and Russia began to recede, we find provisions in the treaties, by which the Christian nations not only recover portions of their territory, but make stipulations for the protection of their fellow-religionists in Turkey.

In the Treaties of Carlowitz, 1699, between Poland and Turkey and Austria and Turkey, there are stipulations for the freedom of the exercise of the Roman Catholic religion, according to the ancient Capitulations ; and power is given to the Christian ambassadors to make complaint if there is any violation of these privileges, or any interference with visits to the Holy Places ; and similar provisions recur in later treaties.[1]

Russia followed suit in the Treaty of Belgrade, 1739, when she stipulated for protection of Russians visiting the Holy Places. By the Treaty of Kainardji, 1774, she took a promise from the Porte to protect the Christian religion and its churches, and again stipulated for the freedom of access to the Holy Places. As the nineteenth century proceeded Russia began to intervene, and was ultimately allowed by Turkey to intervene, for the protection of the Principalities of Serbia and of Moldavia and Wallachia, now called Roumania.

By the Treaty of Bucharest in 1812, Turkey made certain promises for the good government

[1] See Phillimore, *Commentaries on International Law*, vol. i. secs. 412, 413.

of Serbia, which were renewed by the Treaties of Ackerman, 1826, and Adrianople, 1829. .

In 1820 the Greeks rose in revolt. After many years' fighting, Great Britain, France, and Russia, upon the application of Greece, intervened, claiming to have a right to stay the indefinite effusion of blood, and to secure the pacification of the Levant ; and by the Treaty of Adrianople, 1829, Greece was established as a separate State, guaranteed by the Three Powers, Great Britain, France, and Russia.[1] A further Treaty of Establishment and Guarantee when the first King, Otho of Bavaria, was chosen, was made in London, 1832.

By the Treaty of Adrianople, special provision was made with regard to Moldavia and Wallachia.[2] These principalities, which had been conquered by Russia, were restored to Turkey, but in a limited manner only. They were to be placed under the suzerainty of the Porte with stipulations for freedom of worship and independent national government, and full liberty of commerce. The Princes, or Hospodars, were to be elected for life, and there were many other provisions unnecessary to be detailed now. These were modified in the sense of giving further steps towards independence by the Treaty of St. Petersburg,

[1] The position of Greece will be discussed in fuller detail later on.

[2] In extension of similar provisions in the Treaties of Bucharest and Ackerman. The Treaty of Adrianople was confirmed by the Treaty of Peace and Alliance of Unkiar Skelessi in 1833.

in 1834, and again by the Treaty of Balta-Liman in 1849.

In 1853 trouble arose about the rival claims of Latin and Greek Christians to hold religious worship in the Holy Places. France, relying on her Capitulations of 1740, took up the position of Protector of the Roman Catholics; Russia, relying on the Treaty of Kainardji of 1774, took the position of Protector of the Orthodox.

This essay, while it is intended to show the way in which mistaken treaties may bring on war, does not assume to analyse all the causes, even of modern wars.

In the instance of the Crimean War, there was the standing misgovernment of the Christian population by the Porte. There was the contest about the Holy Places, and there were other causes, some of them personal. These are caustically set forth by Kinglake.[1] It is enough here to state that whatever may have been the motives, the pretexts were found in the two treaties last mentioned, and also that the Emperor of Russia thought that by reason of his quasi-protectorate of the Principalities of Moldavia and Wallachia, he could by occupying these principalities make an effective demonstration against Turkey without actually embarking on war.

It is safe to say that but for the embarrassing position in which Turkey was placed by these treaties and engagements, there would have been no Crimean War, even with all the personal

[1] *The Invasion of the Crimea*, vol. i., *passim*.

motives tending to bring about that unhappy and useless strife. It was concluded by the Treaty of Paris of 1856.

That treaty, made between the Five Great Powers of that period and Sardinia and Turkey, has the following provisions :

First, as already stated,[1] it was a Congress Treaty made between Powers, some of whom had not been at war.

Secondly, there was a cession of territory by the Power which on the whole was the vanquished party—Russia. A portion of Bessarabia was ceded to Turkey to be treated as part of the Principality of Moldavia.[2]

There was at the time some reason, real or supposed, for taking away from Russia the control of the Kilia mouth of the Danube. But whatever the reason, this cession, of no serious value to Turkey, or to Europe, produced a disproportionate soreness in Russia, and led to the rather extraordinary result of Roumania—after she had fought on the side of Russia—having to retrocede this territory to Russia in 1878.

By Art. 7 the Porte was admitted to ' participate in the advantages of the public law and system of Europe,' an expression somewhat difficult of comprehension.

This was followed by a promise to respect the independence and territorial integrity of the Ottoman Empire, and a guarantee by the Six Powers in common of the strict observance of

[1] *Vide supra*, p. 12.　　　　　[2] Art. 20.

7

this engagement, and a statement that they would consider any act of violation a question of general interest.

Be it observed that it was a common or collective, and not an individual guarantee, and as no Power other than one of the Six was likely to make a serious attack upon Turkey, there was little value in the guarantee; though no doubt the statement that any attack upon Turkey would be a question of general interest might afford a justification for any one or more of the Six Powers assisting Turkey, in the event of an attack by any of the other Powers.

The vagueness of these provisions and the probability that they would give rise to misunderstanding and bring about war, brings them, it is suggested, under the censure already expressed in an early part of this essay.[1]

By Art. 9 it was stated that note was taken of a communication by the Sultan of the firman which he had issued for the benefit of his Christian subjects, and the firman was welcomed. But it was stipulated that this was to give the Powers no right to interfere collectively, or separately, in the relations of the Sultan with his subjects, or in the internal administration of Turkey.

Thenceforward, any separate interference by France or by Russia was prevented;[2] and indeed

---

[1] *Vide supra*, pp. 7, 8.

[2] Exception should perhaps be made for the pacification of Syria on the occurrence of the conflict between the Druses and the Maronites in 1860, on which occasion France took a prominent part.

even collective interference was apparently forbidden. Nevertheless, from that date till the Russo-Turkish War and the Treaty of Berlin in 1878, the Christian Powers who had come to the assistance of Turkey in the Crimean War and the other Congress Powers felt themselves bound in honour from time to time, as special outbreaks of misgovernment, injustice, and cruelty on the part of the Porte towards its Christian subjects occurred, to offer remonstrances.

They were useless proceedings except in so far as they brought the matter to a climax in 1877 ; and they were useless because the Powers were jealous (and Turkey was aware that they were jealous) of each other ; because if one or two remonstrated without getting the previous concurrence of the others, some of the others at once took the opposite line ; because if all could be brought to an agreement, they could only be brought to agree upon some weak and emasculated course of action ; and because Turkey knew that by apparent compliance with any collective demand she could protect herself against any overt act of interference, while she could put off indefinitely any active measure of compliance, trusting that, however collective was the judgment, there would be no collective, and therefore no effective, execution. Constantinople, under this system, became the fencing school or sparring ground of diplomatists, the weapons being foils with buttons carefully kept on, and fists without the gloves being removed.

Returning to the Treaty, there was a series of useful provisions (Arts. 15 to 19) as to the free navigation of the Danube, adopting the principle as to the navigation of rivers passing through different States which had been codified at the Congress of Vienna in 1815.

And then there were some noteworthy provisions (Arts. 10 to 14) as to the Dardanelles, Bosphorus, and Black Sea.

Here again there must be some retrospect, though only a short one. Though the two Straits are the only highway between the countries bordering on the Black Sea and Sea of Azov and the greater seas of the world, they are so narrow that it seems reasonable that the Sovereign of the adjacent countries should exercise a control over the navigation, in a sense in which it is not exercised by Great Britain and France over the Straits of Dover, nor even by Denmark and Sweden over the Sound; and States generally have been more concerned to provide for, than to question, this control.

Russia, at any rate, up to this date was more anxious to prevent ships of war of hostile Powers from entering the Black Sea than to get her own out. Other nations were more anxious to keep Russian ships of war in than to have the opportunity of attacking her coasts in the Black Sea.

And, accordingly, in treaties from time to time other States have, so to speak, kept the Porte up to its duty. Thus, by the Treaty of Constantinople of 1809, between Great Britain and

Turkey—concluded after the English Fleet had been sent to Constantinople on a warlike errand—'the ancient rule of the Ottoman Empire' as to ships of war of other nations coming into the two Straits was recognised.

By the Treaty of Adrianople 1829 (Art. 7), freedom of navigation for merchant vessels proceeding to or from Russia was stipulated. But the Clause was confined to merchant vessels.

By the Secret Article annexed to the Treaty of Unkiar Skelessi of 1833, Turkey was to close the Dardanelles against any foreign ship of war of a Power engaged in hostilities with Russia. This was a treaty of defensive alliance between Russia and Turkey ; and this particular provision was to be a contribution on the part of Turkey, taking the place of any other material assistance. As soon as it was known it was protested against by France ; and it probably led to the Treaty of July 1841 between the Five Powers and Turkey, in which the Sultan declared his firm resolution to maintain the principle invariably established as the ancient rule of his Empire, by virtue of which vessels of war of foreign Powers are forbidden to enter into the two Straits, saying that as long as he is at peace he would not admit any vessel of war into the Straits ; and the Five Powers, on the other hand, engaged to respect this determination of the Sultan, and to conform to the principle thus announced.[1]

[1] Upon the occasion of the Convention of London in July 1840 between Great Britain, Austria, Prussia, Russia, and Turkey, for

By Art. 10 of the Treaty of Paris and a separate Convention annexed to the treaty, these provisions as to the closing of the Straits to ships of war in time of war [1] is renewed, notwithstanding that experience had shown that it was open to some objection, because if Turkey anticipated war with Russia, she could not protect herself by bringing the vessels of her Allies within the Dardanelles without committing an act which might be taken as the opening of hostilities; and this had been one of the steps by which the nations had drifted into the Crimean War.

Notwithstanding the approach of the British and French Fleets, the Russians had been able at a very early stage of the war to destroy a Turkish Fleet at Sinope. And this act, though warrantable because the two Powers were already at war, was—owing to the imperfect means of communication then in existence — supposed by the British public to have been done in time of peace, and to be an act, as it was called, of treachery

the Pacification of the Levant and the defence of Constantinople against Mehemet Ali, which might necessitate the entrance of vessels of war of some of the Four Powers into the Straits, there had been a provision for their entrance in these exceptional circumstances, with a statement of the general rule as mentioned in the text. There was an exception in the Treaty of 1841, for light vessels employed in the service of the Legations, and this is repeated in the Treaty of 1856, with a further provision for police vessels for the Danube.

[1] But it was provided that the Porte might ' open the said Straits in time of peace to the vessels of war of friendly or allied Powers, in case the Sublime Porte should judge it necessary in order to secure the execution of the stipulations of the Treaty of Paris.'

on the part of Russia. The writer is just old enough to remember the sensation which that destruction produced.

It was thought to guard against this, and accordingly Arts. 11, 13, and 14 were inserted in the Treaty of Paris. By Art. 11 :

The Black Sea is neutralised : its waters and its ports, thrown open to the mercantile marine of every nation, are formally and in perpetuity interdicted to the flag of war, either of the Powers possessing its coasts, or of any other Power, with the exceptions mentioned in Articles 14 and 19 of the present Treaty.[1]

Art. 12 provided for freedom of commerce. Arts. 13 and 14 are as follows :

Art 13. The Black Sea being neutralised according to the terms of Art. 11, the maintenance or establishment upon its coast of military-maritime arsenals becomes alike unnecessary and purposeless ; in consequence, his Majesty the Emperor of All the Russias and his Imperial Majesty the Sultan engage not to establish or to maintain upon that coast any military-maritime arsenal.

Art 14. Their Majesties the Emperor of All the Russias and the Sultan, having concluded a Convention for the purpose of settling the force and the number of light vessels, necessary for the service of their coasts, which they reserve to themselves to maintain in the Black Sea, that Convention is annexed to the present Treaty, and shall have the same force and validity as if it formed an integral part thereof. It cannot be either annulled or modified without the assent of the Powers signing the present Treaty.

This is an example, as the late Sir Robert Phillimore used to say, of one of the worst forms

---

[1] Light vessels used by the Legations and police vessels for the Danube.

of restriction of sovereignty or imposition of servitude known in the history of treaties, sinning against Maxims 4 and 5.[1]

It was so irritating and offensive to Russia that she took the first opportunity during the Franco-German War of claiming to have it cancelled; and by the Treaty of London of 1871, Arts. 11, 13, and 14 of the Treaty of Paris and the special Convention annexed, were abrogated, and in lieu there was inserted a simple statement that the ' Black Sea remains open as heretofore to the mercantile marine of all nations.'

There had been no war, nor, it is believed, any threat of war between Russia and Turkey during the interval. Whether the existence of these Articles had been any factor in preventing war can hardly be determined.

What did happen was that the way in which Russia sought to have these clauses abrogated, and the pretensions which she put forward, had to be met by a special Protocol providing that it is ' an essential principle of the law of nations that none of them can liberate itself from the engagements of a Treaty, nor modify the stipulations thereof, unless with the consent of the contracting parties by means of an amicable understanding.' What is to be arranged as to these Straits and as to the Black Sea in the Peace after the present War seems to the writer a most difficult problem.[2]

There was in the Treaty of Paris a hopeful

---

[1] *Vide supra*, p. 4.   [2] *Vide infra*, Chapter VIII.
[3] *Vide infra*, Chapter IX.

Article (Art. 8) by which, in case of any mis-understanding between Turkey and any of the signing Powers, each party agreed that the other Powers should have an opportunity of mediating. This matter was developed in the twenty-third Protocol into an expression of a wish that all States should have, before appealing to arms, recourse, as far as circumstances might allow, to the good offices of a friendly Power,[1] and this may be taken as the beginning of those Treaties of Arbitration which, while by no means the panacea that sanguine people expected, have yet done some good work.

By Arts. 22 and 27 of the Treaty of Paris, the positions of Moldavia and Wallachia were regulated, and their organisation was placed under the collective guarantee of the contracting Powers; and by Art. 28, the rights of Serbia were placed under a similar guarantee, except that as to the Danubian Principalities the control of the Porte is described as suzerainty, while no such expression is used with respect to Serbia. But in both cases the sovereignty of Turkey was more or less impaired by international contract with the Six Powers, as it had been impaired by contract with Russia in previous times.

It may well be that in dealing with the par-ticular circumstances of the case, it was necessary to have a gradual emancipation of the provinces pre-eminently Christian from the dominion of the

---

[1] *International Tribunals*, by W. Evans Darby, LL.D;, pp. 299, 300.

Porte ; and Treaties of Guarantee, almost amount-
ing to the creation of Protectorates, may in these
cases be justified.

But it is plain that the position was that of a
halfway house towards independence, and that
the partial derogation of sovereignty would in
time end in an absolute loss ; and the difficulty
of a collective guarantee or protectorate is well
shown by what happened to Moldavia and
Wallachia.[1] They were intended to be separate
Principalities with separate Princes or Hospodars.

A further Convention as to these Principalities
had to be made in 1858, between the Six Powers
and Turkey, which advanced them a step further
on the road towards independence. In 1859,
a somewhat reluctant Conference at Paris recognised Prince Couza as Hospodar of both Principalities. And in 1866 the two Principalities
again chose the same Prince—Prince Charles of
Hohenzollern—and notwithstanding some dislike
on the part of the signing Powers and much
unwillingness on the part of Turkey, his title
had to be recognised, and the two Principalities
became one, soon to be called Roumania, and to
procure its independence by the Treaty of Berlin,
1878 (Art. 43), and become a kingdom later, in
May, 1881.[2]

As has been already indicated, the European

---

[1] As to suzerainty, see a valuable treatise by Dr. Charles
Stubbs, 1882.

[2] There was a further treaty between the Six Powers and
Turkey enlarging the rights of Serbia, 1862,

Provinces of Turkey remained in an unsettled and unhappy condition.

At last revolts in Bosnia and Bulgaria, put down—in the latter case at any rate—with circumstances of great atrocity by Turkey, led to Serbia declaring war, for the sake of her co-nationalists and co-religionists, in 1876. On March 31, 1877, the Six Great Powers formulated a Protocol in which they agreed upon the conditions which should be applied to Christians in Turkey and on reforms to be made in Bosnia and Herzegovina, and Bulgaria. The Porte met this by a protest on April 9 ; and the Powers as a collective body were not prepared to go further than words. So Russia, on April 24, declared war against Turkey, and Roumania declared her Independence on June 3, and joined forces with Russia.

As Russia began to be successful the Ministers of Great Britain were alarmed ; and on January 14, 1878, the British Ambassador at St. Petersburg communicated a Memorandum to the effect that :

Any Treaty concluded between the Governments of Russia and the Porte affecting the Treaties of 1856 and 1871 must be a European Treaty, and would not be valid without the assent of the Powers who were parties to those Treaties.

On March 3, 1878, Russia and Turkey concluded the Peace of San Stefano. Thereupon, as Great Britain had already required, but upon the formal demand of Austria, the Six Powers and Turkey met in Congress at Berlin, and the Treaty of Berlin, July 13, 1878, was made. This war and this peace constitute the second source from which the flood of the present trouble has sprung.

The treaty did not produce a state of rest in Turkey. It went too far for Turkish absolutism and not far enough in relieving the Christians and disposing of the claims of the various competing Christian nationalities and churches.

It may be fairly said that the changes made by the Treaty of Berlin were so vast that it was impossible to foresee the results in all their bearings, and that the stipulations of the treaty were necessarily temporary and provisional. But there are other objections to be made. The Five Great Powers who intervened between Russia and Turkey professed to enter upon the negotiations with the object of securing the Balance of Power, and of providing for the welfare of the oppressed populations, while reconciling with these objects the legitimate claims of Russia as a victorious belligerent. But in the result it proved that several of the Powers were not so disinterested.

Russia acquired as her compensation a considerable increase of territory in Asia, fettered by a provision as to the port of Batoum—a fetter which she shook off on July 5, 1886. She acquired also, nominally from Turkey but practically from her own Ally Roumania, portions of Bessarabia which she had ceded in 1856.

Of the other Five Great Powers, Great Britain, who had been the first to interpose to deprive Russia of the fruits of her victory, was found to have made her own bargain with Turkey.

By a Convention of June 24, 1878, made between her and Turkey, it was agreed that in the event of Russia insisting upon retaining certain of her conquests in Asia Minor, Great Britain should enter into a defensive alliance with Turkey protecting the residue of her Asiatic territory. Then follow these words :

> In return, his Imperial Majesty the Sultan promises to England to introduce necessary reforms, to be agreed upon later between the two Powers, into the government, and for the protection of the Christian and other subjects of the Porte in these territories ; and in order to enable England to make necessary provision for executing her engagement his Imperial Majesty the Sultan further consents to assign the Island of Cyprus to be occupied and administered by England.

There was an annex to this treaty by which it was provided that Great Britain should pay to the Sultan as a quasi-tribute a sum equal to the then nett revenues of the island.

Russia, as it was expected, did insist upon retaining her Asiatic conquests, and so Cyprus passed to Great Britain. It was not a large acquisition, but still the acquisition removed Great Britain from the category of disinterested Powers. She was never called upon to fulfil her part of the Convention, as, by an irony of fate, she has ended by being at war with Turkey, and helping Russia to conquer the Turkish provinces in Asia.

As to the Porte performing its part of the contract, the massacres of the Armenians afford the only known answer. It is to be hoped that, when diplomatic secrets are revealed, it will be found that the statesmen of Great Britain made some use of the power of interference on behalf of the oppressed races which the Convention certainly gave them.

Next comes Austria. She obtained the right to occupy Bosnia and Herzegovina, of which more hereafter.

France made no immediate gain. It is said that when her Ministers complained of the bargain as to Cyprus, they were told that they might acquire in their turn a position in Tunis. This was obtained by France in 1881.

There remain as disinterested Powers only Italy and Germany. Italy has since acquired Tripoli. Germany contented herself with the policy of peaceful penetration, and has not unnaturally reaped her reward in the friendship and alliance of Turkey.

It would now be convenient to deal with the clauses of this, the last great European Treaty.

First, as to Bulgaria. In the Treaty of San Stefano it was proposed that she should form a large State stretching from the Danube over the Balkans into Macedonia, reaching the Ægean and including much territory now forming part of Serbia or of Greece. The Powers, in their wisdom, thought that this would be creating too powerful a Dependency of Russia ; and so Bulgaria was converted into two quasi-States—Bulgaria Proper, which was to occupy a position similar to that intended to be occupied by Roumania and Serbia, and Eastern Roumelia, a much reduced area to the south of the Balkans to be administered by a Governor-General for Turkey, and with less autonomy than the tributary States. It is not necessary now to discuss these somewhat subtle distinctions which were rapidly obliterated. The two areas are provided for in the first twenty-one Articles of the Treaty. Bulgaria was to pay tribute.

There were a number of constitutional provisions, one being that the Prince should be freely elected by the population and confirmed by the Sublime Porte with the consent of the Powers. No member of any of the reigning Houses of the Great European Powers could be elected Prince.

Art. 5 contained provisions which were introduced almost in the same words into the Constitution of Bulgaria, Serbia, and Montenegro, and in a stronger form into that of Roumania. All these States seem to have been considered as in leading strings and not to be trusted to work out their own liberties. As an expression of what is desirable, of what diplomatists call a *vœu*, these provisions are admirable. If it was intended to give any of the Treaty Powers a right to enforce them, they would afford ground for very mischievous interference.

The language is as follows :

. . . the following points shall form the basis of the public law of Bulgaria :

A difference of religious beliefs or confessions shall not exclude or incapacitate any person from the enjoyment of civil and political rights, admission to public appointments, functions, or honours, or from the exercise of the various professions and employments, in any district whatever.

Liberty, and the public exercise of all religions, shall be assured to all persons belonging to Bulgaria, as well as to strangers, and no obstacle shall be interposed either to the hierarchical organisation of the different communions, or to their connection with their spiritual heads.

The fine spun plans for dividing and weakening Bulgaria were of little avail. Prince Alexander of Battenberg,[1] the first Prince of Bulgaria, succeeded in acquiring possession of Eastern Roumelia. Bulgaria became involved in war with Serbia from November 14, 1885, to March 3, 1886 ; and on April 5, 1886, the Powers recognised the inevitable and saved their faces by purporting, with the assent of Turkey, to entrust the Governor-Generalship of Eastern Roumelia to Prince Alexander.

Prince Alexander was succeeded by Prince Ferdinand of Saxe Coburg.[2] Matters were in a very uncertain state for some time ; but in 1896 the latter was formally appointed by the Sultan —with the consent of the Great Powers—Prince and Governor-General ; and on October 5, 1908, he publicly proclaimed that the two provinces were united, and made himself independent King, paying an indemnity to Turkey in lieu of the tribute and of taxes.

Greece comes next in the order of the treaty, but it would be convenient to postpone her case.

[1] Elected July 27, 1879, dethroned August 21, 1886.
[2] Elected August 14, 1887.

By Art. 25, it is provided that :

> The Provinces of Bosnia and Herzegovina shall be occupied and administered by Austria-Hungary. The Government of Austria-Hungary, not desiring to undertake the administration of the Sandjak of Novi-Bazar, which extends between Servia and Montenegro in a south-easterly direction to the other side of Mitrovitza, the Ottoman administration will remain in force there. Notwithstanding, in order to assure the maintenance of the new political state of affairs as well as freedom and security of communications, Austria-Hungary reserves the right of keeping garrisons and having military and commercial roads in the whole of this part of the ancient Vilayet of Bosnia. With this object the Governments of Austria-Hungary and Turkey reserve to themselves to come to an understanding as to the details.

This arrangement was made without consultation of the population and without any consideration for it. The two provinces are occupied by a South Slavonic population, partly Roman Catholic, partly Mohammedan, but mainly belonging to the Orthodox Church. Those of the two latter religions certainly resented their subjection to Austria; and their opposition was put down with much violence and bloodshed, the Austrians having a very heavy hand.

In 1908, Austria, with hardly any pretext to cover her action, affected to turn her occupation into complete sovereignty, and to annex the provinces to her Empire. It had been expressly stipulated in an agreement signed by the Austro-Hungarian and Ottoman Plenipotentiaries at Berlin, that when the good administration of the provinces had been established, they should be evacuated by Austria and restored to Turkey.

8

The annexation was a flagrant breach of this agreement. Naturally, Austria-Hungary has been uneasy ever since. Naturally, she has dreaded the tendency of the Slavonic population to gravitate towards Serbia. Not unnaturally, she suspected Serbian agents of having a part in the massacre of the Archduke in 1914. Hence her outrageous demands upon Serbia which formed the pretext of the present war.

Montenegro is the subject of Arts. 26 to 33. She was already an independent State, but her independence was now formally recognised. The same condition as to religious freedom was imposed upon her as upon the new States, and she was given an increase of territory. But the Sandjak of Novi-bazar was carefully preserved to Turkey, so as to prevent any union between Serbia and Montenegro, and any formation of an important South Slavonic State. This again was due to the jealousy of Austria-Hungary.

Serbia was recognised as an independent Principality and her status was provided for in the same way, by Arts. 34 to 42, and she was to bear a portion of the public debt of Turkey.

Roumania was made independent conditionally upon her restoring Bessarabian territory to Russia, and upon her complying with the terms of Art. 44, which is as follows :

Art. 44. In Roumania the difference of religious creeds and confessions shall not be alleged against any person as a ground for exclusion or incapacity in matters relating to the enjoyment of civil and political rights, admission to public employments, functions, and honours, or the exercise of various professions and industries in any locality whatsoever.

The freedom and outward exercise of all forms of worship will be assured to all persons belonging to the Roumanian State, as well as to foreigners, and no hindrance shall be offered either to the hierarchical organisation of the different communions, or to their relations with their spiritual chiefs.

The nationals of all the Powers, traders or others, shall be treated in Roumania without distinction of creed, on a footing of perfect equality.[1]

She and the navigation of the Danube are the subjects of Arts. 43 to 57 of the treaty.

Arts. 58 to 60 relate to the cession by Turkey of territories in Asia to Russia.

By Art. 61, which deals with the unhappy Armenians :

The Sublime Porte undertakes to carry out without further delay the improvements and reforms demanded by local requirements in the provinces inhabited by the Circassians and Kurds.

It will periodically make known the steps taken to this effect to the Powers who will superintend their application.

By Art. 62 :

The Sublime Porte having expressed the intention to maintain the principle of religious liberty and give it the widest scope, the Contracting Parties take note of this spontaneous declaration.

Then come details as to religious liberty, equal political rights, Christian evidence before tribunals, protection of ecclesiastics, representa-

[1] Comment has already been made on this provision. It may be added that as to the Jews, whom it was intended to protect, it was futile.

tions by diplomatists and consular agents, with a saving of the rights of France and her *status quo* in the Holy Places, and the rights and prerogatives of all monks of Mount Athos. No doubt foreign ecclesiastics and the specially protected monks have been allowed to enjoy the benefit of these provisions. But as to the Christian subjects of the Porte in Macedonia and the Armenians in Asia, their lot remained as hard and in some cases harder than ever. Such clauses, as has been already observed, are useless if not mischievous.

By Art. 63, the Treaties of 1856 and 1871 were, so far as they were not abrogated or modified, confirmed.

Now as to Greece. A protocol of Feb. 3, 1830, intervening between the Treaties of Adrianople, 1829, and London, 1832, had given her a restricted territory which was in principle unjustifiable, and a frontier which was absurd.[1] She had been strengthened by the acquisition of the Ionian Islands, as already mentioned; and in respect of them, as well as of her original territory, she remained as under the protectorate and guarantee of Great Britain, France, and Russia.

By Art. 24 of the Treaty of Berlin, provision was made for what was called a rectification of frontier, which was in fact to give her Thessaly and a portion of Epirus.

---

[1] Leopold, afterwards King of the Belgians, refused the kingdom of Greece, because of these narrow limits, and because Crete did not form part of the proposed kingdom. There is a good general article on Greece in the *Encyclopædia Britannica*.

The greatest difficulties arose about this. The Six Powers, whose mediation had been provided for, had to fix the boundary themselves, and to compel its acceptance by Turkey by force. Eventually, the boundary was settled in 1881.

When Bulgaria became united, Greek feeling was roused and the Greeks had to be kept quiet by what was called ' a peaceful blockade,' a very anomalous operation established by several of the Great Powers in 1886. Then the Cretan difficulty arose.

By Art. 23 the Sultan undertook ' scrupulously to apply in the Island of Crete the organic law of 1868, while introducing into it the modifications which may be considered equitable.' And there were further stipulations which it is unnecessary to mention, because the Porte never intended to perform them, and did not in fact perform them.

The Cretans rose in insurrection in 1907, and the Greeks declared war upon Turkey. They were beaten and had to cede a small portion of the territory that they had gained in 1881, and pay an indemnity. Crete was then put under a High Commissioner. Prince George of Greece was made High Commissioner ; and since Crete has been annexed to Greece.

All these developments of the Treaty of Berlin —the formation of a united Bulgaria, the struggle between Serbia and Bulgaria, and the enlargement of Greece—left those, which it is convenient to call ' the Balkan Powers,' and the national aspirations of their peoples still unsatisfied, and in October, 1912, the Balkan League, consisting of Bulgaria, Greece, Montenegro, and Serbia, declared war upon Turkey, and after a victorious campaign received considerable accessions of territory by the Peace of May 30, 1913.

Unfortunately, however, disputes arose between Bulgaria on the one side, and Greece and Serbia on the other, which led to a war between them, breaking out on June 30, and concluded by a Peace at Bucharest on August 6. Roumania came into this war as against Bulgaria, and the result was that Bulgaria lost all round. The Turks took the opportunity of recovering Adrianople, which they had been forced to cede to her. Roumania took Silistria and a considerable further portion of the Dobrudja from her; and Serbia and Greece obtained in substance what they had demanded at her expense.

The soreness which was left has led to Bulgaria joining in the attack upon Serbia made in the present war, and becoming the Ally of Germany, Austria-Hungary, and her old enemy Turkey. On the other hand, Greece, who had entered into a defensive alliance with Serbia as against Bulgaria, when called upon by Serbia for her assistance, replied, rightly or wrongly, that the *casus fœderis* had not arisen, and refused to help her; and though Greece owes her origin and her growth in 1881, and her deliverance from Turkey when she was beaten in 1897, to the three Powers, Great Britain, France, and Russia; the accretion of her territory by the Ionian Islands

to Great Britain; and the pecuniary appanage
of her Sovereign to the generosity of the three
Powers, she under her late king had to be com-
pelled by force to remain neutral and abstain
from helping the enemies of the three Powers.[1]

If the Greater Bulgaria provided by the Treaty
of San Stefano had been left, the arrangement
might have been injurious to the Serbian and
Greek nationalities, but as between Bulgaria and
Turkey it would only have been an anticipation of
what happened in 1912. There would probably
have been no war in 1912, and very likely no War
of Partition between the Balkan States in 1913.
The Western Provinces of Turkey, separated by
Greater Bulgaria, would have naturally fallen to
Serbia, Greece, and Montenegro, with perhaps a
separate Principality of Albania.[2]

The half-measure of the Treaty of Paris in
1856 brought constant unrest and ever-increasing
strife till the Russo-Turkish war of 1877. The
further half-measures of the Treaty of Berlin
in 1878 left their legacy of strife and warfare,
which was only partially settled by the Treaty
of 1913, and is, as has already been said, one of
the principal causes of the present War. Next
time the position of the Balkan States should
be decisively and finally settled.

[1] The abdication of Constantine, King of Greece, is already
leading to different results.

[2] The author of *Nationalism and the War in the Near East*
(Carnegie Endowment for International Peace, Oxford, 1915)
also takes this view. See pp. 72, 73.

CHAPTER VI

EXTRA-EUROPEAN TREATIES OF PEACE

THE United States of America have had few wars. Confederations, as a rule, do not fight. Their entry into the present War is the more noteworthy.

They have had two great internal struggles, one during the War of Independence and the other during the War of Secession; and they have had two wars against Great Britain, the War of Independence and the War of 1812. They have had wars with Mexico and one with Spain; and they entered into military operations, which were not precisely war, against Japan, ending happily in a Treaty of Commerce in 1854.

The Treaty of Versailles in 1783, which established their independence, does not afford many subjects of comment. It was a treaty of recognition, not of future stipulations.

Notice has already been taken of the difficulties which were experienced in drawing the boundaries between the United States and Canada, as so much of the boundary passed at that time through unsurveyed land.[1]

[1] *Vide supra*, pp. 7, 31.

The other matter in the treaty is that of Fisheries. Great Britain consented generously but unwisely to give to the fishermen of the United States special rights of fishing in British North American waters; and their rights have been the subject of pretty frequent dispute. Further provision had to be made for them in a treaty of 1818 and again in 1854. They were a matter of arbitration at the same time as the more important *Alabama* claims and San Juan boundary dispute in 1871. In 1907 a *Modus Vivendi*, as it was called, a temporary arrangement, was established by Convention; and finally, in 1909, the parties went again to Arbitration. This is a strong example of the objections to such obligations.

The Treaty of Ghent, 1814, was in substance a restoration of the *status quo ante*, and calls for no special mention here, except that there is an interesting stipulation that Great Britain shall come to terms with the warring Indian tribes, and a declaration against the Slave Trade.

The War with Mexico in 1846–1848 ended in the cession by the latter of Texas, New Mexico, and Northern California, in return for a money payment by the United States.

There were later Boundary Treaties with Mexico in 1853 and 1884; but there are no special provisions calling for remark, except that in 1853 the United States stipulated for a right of free transit from one ocean to the other across the Isthmus of Tehuantepec.

Important as the war was with Spain, large as were the American gains and the Spanish losses, there are no special lessons to be drawn from the Treaty of Paris, 1898, which brought the war to a conclusion. The treaty recorded the conquests of the United States. Spain ceded what she had lost. Porto Rico, Guam in the Ladrone Islands, and the Philippine Islands were ceded to the United States. (Arts. 2 and 3.)

As to Cuba, there was an unusual provision. Spain relinquished her sovereignty, but there was no cession to the United States. Only it was provided that the United States should occupy the island for the time and protect life and property. (Art. 1.) This was because the United States were not going to annex Cuba, but to constitute a dependent and protected Republic, an arrangement which was effected by a treaty of 1903 between the two Republics.

As to details, there are some instructive clauses in the Treaty of Paris which future diplomatists may note. In lieu of the usual clauses providing for indemnities to private persons, each State relinquished all claims to indemnity, national or individual. (Art. 7.)

' Spanish subjects, natives of the Peninsula '— *i.e.*, Spaniards proper—might remove themselves or their goods, or could remain in the ceded territories and yet preserve their allegiance to Spain if they made a formal declaration. (Art. 9.) By Art. 10, ' The inhabitants of the territories over which Spain relinquishes or cedes her Sovereignty shall be secured in the free exercise of their religion.'

It is curious that the usual clause stipulating Peace and Amity does not appear in this treaty. But there was a supplementary Treaty of Peace and Friendship in 1902 dealing with general relations between the two States, by Art. 29 of which all treaties prior to the Treaty of Paris (except the Treaty of February 17, 1834) were to be deemed annulled.

Mexico has twice provoked wars with European Powers by her injuries to subjects of those States and her refusal or inability to make redress. But the writer is not aware that there is anything in the subsequent Treaties of Peace which calls for remark. The ill-fated expedition of the Emperor Maximilian, under the encouragement of Napoleon III., was brought to a close as far as France was concerned by the simple withdrawal of her forces ; and Maximilian was put to death by Juarez in 1867.

Many of the European Powers have been nearly at war with Venezuela. Great Britain had a serious dispute about territory which, through the medium of the United States, was referred to arbitration in 1897.

In 1903, a number of States had claims for compensation which it was obvious that Venezuela would be unable to meet in full. Some had claims to preferential treatment ; and this question was by common assent referred to the Tribunal at The Hague, which decided in 1904 that these claims were entitled to preference.

Since the States of Central and South America fought for and obtained their independence of Spain, they do not seem to have been at actual war with any European Power.

Treaties of Peace with Asiatic Powers generally proceed on such different lines that they would not be helpful for the purposes of this work. But there are two Treaties of Peace to which Japan has been a party, proceeding upon modern and European lines, which therefore should be mentioned.

The last war (the only one of modern days) between Japan and China was brought to an end by the Treaty of Shimonoseki, 1895. Its provisions were characterised by much simplicity. The cause of the war was the claim of China to the suzerainty of Corea. Art. 1 of the treaty declared the complete independence of Corea. Arts. 2, 3, and 4 provided for the compensation of Japan in territory and money. The ceded territory comprised the Peninsula of Fengtsen upon the Continent of Asia, the Island of Formosa, and the Pescadores Islands.

The acquisition of the Peninsula was subsequently abandoned by Japan in deference to the remonstrances of Russia, Germany, and France. But this action, on the part of Russia especially, was bitterly felt in Japan, and became one of the causes of the Russo-Japanese War. In Art. 5 the usual modern European provision as to the inhabitants of the ceded territory was adopted. They were allowed a period (in this case two years) to dispose of their lands and remove themselves and their goods. If they remained after that period they became Japanese subjects. In Art. 6 the vexed juridical question whether war puts an end to previous treaties was solved [1] by declaring that in this case it had done so ; and provision was made for a new treaty of commerce and navigation, and regulation of frontier lines. China contracted also to open certain ports to the Japanese. Art. 8 provided an instance of the victor taking a material guarantee for the conditions which he exacted. The Japanese were temporarily to occupy Wei Hai Wei.

The remaining Arts. 7, 9, 10, relate to the exchange of prisoners, the evacuation of territories, and the cessation of hostilities.[2] When the prisoners on both sides were restored, China promised not to maltreat or punish her own subjects given back to her by Japan. She engaged also to release all Japanese accused of espionage or military offences, and not to punish any of her subjects who might have compromised themselves by their relations with the Japanese during the war.

If any of her African colonies should be restored to Germany, it would be well to follow the precedent set by this last clause, which is an extension of the usual form.[3]

The Treaty of Portsmouth, 1905, between Japan

---

[1] *Vide infra*, Chapter VIII.

[2] See the Treaty in Ariga, *La Guerre Sino-Japonaise*. Paris, 1896.　　　　　[3] *Vide infra*, Chapter IX.

and Russia, was of a much less usual stamp. Professor Ariga remarks that it would require a volume to consider all the questions which it raises.[1] The land war was fought in Manchuria, which was neither Russian nor Japanese, but Chinese. It is true that Russia had a lease from China of Port Arthur and other territorial rights; and this war showed (as does the present war in which the Japanese have besieged and taken the territory leased to Germany by China) what complications such a form of territorial sovereignty brings with it. Hence, in the Treaty of Portsmouth there was, strictly speaking, only one cession of territory, that was the cession of half the Island of Sakhaline by Russia to Japan; but if actualities are looked at, Russia lost and Japan gained (always it was provided with the consent of China) Port Arthur and the railway and the mines; and the consent of China being necessary, each of the contracting parties engaged that it would procure this consent.

Further, the Japanese gave an assurance, as if Port Arthur were their own, that the rights of Russians to their property there should be respected. (Arts. 5 and 6.) Then each agreed by Art. 3 to evacuate Chinese territory and to restore it to China, while Russia declared that she had no pretensions which would interfere with Chinese sovereignty. By Art. 4 each undertook not to interfere with the measures which China might take to develop Manchuria;

[1] Ariga, *La Guerre Russo-Japonaise.* Paris, 1908.

and Arts. 7 and 8 provided for the regulation of *their* railways in Manchuria.

So that the treaty sometimes appears as if it were made for the benefit of China, though she is no party to it, sometimes as if there were no China, or as if she need not be consulted as to Manchuria.

Art. 2 dealt with Corea. Russia, recognising that Japan possessed 'predominant interests, political, military, and economic,' engaged not to intervene or put any obstacle in the way of any measures of direction, protection, or control, which the Japanese Government might consider it necessary to take in Corea.[1]

This treaty adopted the same juridical rule that former treaties were to be considered as having been annulled by the war, but provided that till there was a new Treaty of Commerce each State should be treated by the other on the footing of the most favoured nation. (Art. 12.) There was the usual clause (Art. 10) providing for the inhabitants of the ceded territory ; but, contrary to the usual custom, those who continued to reside did not become Japanese

---

[1] The treaty was signed in French and English, but if there was any divergence the French text was to prevail. Professor Ariga gives the French text, and it is well to give it here :

'Le Gouvernement Impérial de Russie, reconnaissant que le Japon posséde en Corée des intérêts prédominants politiques, militaires et économiques, s'engage à ne point intervenir ni mettre d'obstacle aux mesures de direction, de protection et de contrôle que le Gouvernement Impérial de Japon pourrait considérer nécessaires de prendre en Corée.'

Some supplementary provisions follow.

subjects; and Japan might require them to leave the country.

The expense of the keep of prisoners on both sides was to be calculated, and Russia which had taken the fewer prisoners was to pay the difference. This is a useful provision, which might be remembered when the new treaty is prepared.

By this treaty, as has been said, ' the paramount political, military, and economic interests' of Japan in Corea were recognised by Russia, as they were recognised by Great Britain in her Treaty of Alliance with Japan of the same year. This recognition of predominant influence is, like the phrase 'sphere of influence' in the Berlin Act of 1885, as to Africa, and in the Convention between Great Britain and Germany of 1890, as to spheres of influence in East, West, and Southwest Africa, as far as the writer's knowledge goes, a modern provision in diplomacy. But the principle underlying it is not wholly new, though generally applied to the case of small States in a special relation with their immediate great neighbour, such as Ragusa with Venice ; Geneva, before she became a complete part of the Swiss Confederation, with France ; Monaco, first with Sardinia and then after the cession of the County of Nice, with France ; Nepaul with Great Britain.

Recently similar arrangements of mutual recognition of spheres of influence have been made between Great Britain and France as to Siam in 1904, and Great Britain and Russia as to Persia in 1907. In these cases there is the remarkable result that the spheres of influence cut another, presumably independent, State into two.[1]

As to Corea, the effect of China yielding up her claims to suzerainty, and of Russia and Great Britain's recognising the predominant interests of Japan, is that she has been, as any one would have predicted, annexed by Japan, with very doubtful benefit to her people.

The African treaties are also outside the scope of this essay; and the important ones are not Treaties of Peace, that is, treaties concluding war.

But there are certain Congress treaties of such value as having hitherto prevented war, that there should be a brief mention of them.

The Berlin Act, February 26, 1885, which was signed by fourteen Powers, provided for freedom of trade in the basin of the Congo, the neutrality of the territories in its basin, the navigation of the Congo and of the Niger, and rules for future occupation of African territory. It recognised the division of a great part of Africa into European possessions, protectorates, and 'spheres of influence,' the phrase which has just been mentioned. On August 1 of the same year the King of the Belgians notified his possession of the Congo State and took the title of Sovereign of the Independent State of the Congo.[2] The Berlin Act did its best to provide

---

[1] In the case of Siam the division is into three parts: basin of Mekong, French; and basin of Salwin, British; while the basin of Meenan is claimed by neither.

[2] The State was ceded to Belgium in 1907.

9

for the neutrality of the Congo State by the following Article. (Chap. 2, Art. iii.)

> In case a Power exercising rights of Sovereignty or Protectorate in the countries mentioned in Art. 1 (Basin of the Congo as defined) and placed under the Free Trade system, shall be involved in war, then the High Signatory Parties to this present Act and those who shall hereafter adopt it, bind themselves to lend their good offices, in order that the territories belonging to this Power and comprised in the Conventional free trade zone shall, by the common consent of this Power and of the other belligerent or belligerents, be placed during the war under the rule of neutrality and considered as belonging to a non-belligerent State, the belligerents thenceforth abstaining from extending hostilities to the territories thus neutralised and from using them as a base for warlike operations.

And the King of the Belgians in his proclamation of August 1, 1885, claimed the benefit of this Article. Needless to say that as the neutrality of Belgium has not been respected in the present War, the Congo State has also been involved, notwithstanding this provision.

On July 1, 1890, Great Britain and Germany entered into a Convention regulating their respective spheres of influence in East, West, and South-west Africa, and Germany recognised the Protectorate of Great Britain over those dominions of the Sultan of Zanzibar which were not to be ceded to Germany—as certain portions of the Sultan's territory were in the following October.

This was the occasion when Great Britain ceded to Germany Heligoland, the island which she had conquered from Denmark in the Napoleonic

Wars, and kept at the Peace of 1815, because it had been so valuable to her, but which she in 1890 deemed of small value, little reckoning of its future terrible importance.

France also in 1890 recognised Great Britain's Protectorate of Zanzibar. In 1904 France and Great Britain exchanged recognitions of each other's respective peculiar interests in Morocco and Egypt, and Spain adhered to this declaration. Finally, in 1906, there was a general treaty, to which the Six Great Powers, Belgium, the Netherlands, Spain, Portugal, Sweden, the United States, and Morocco were parties, regulating the affairs of this latter country. Though she had been a party to this Treaty, Germany by her aggression at Agadir nearly precipitated war in 1911, and showed to the statesmen of France, at any rate, if not to others, that its advent was only the matter of a few years.

CHAPTER VII

TREATIES CONCERNING THE LAWS OF WAR

THE laws of war may be divided into two classes—those which provide for fair and regulated fighting between belligerents,[1] and those which provide for the relations between belligerents and neutrals. The first class may be subdivided as follows : There are those unwritten laws which have existed as long as there has been any formal warfare of which we know in history, such as that a flag of truce must be respected ; that a prisoner whose surrender has been accepted must not be put to death, at any rate immediately and without trial ; that a spy is liable to instant execution. These are elementary cases and are only given as instances.

Secondly, there are treaties between pairs of nations, making written laws as between themselves or providing for concessions from the strict laws of war, which they engage to make to each other in the event of their ever being at war. Thirdly, international conventions making written laws for the greater part of the world.

[1] See Sir T. E. Holland's book, *The Laws of War on Land.*

The defect of all these laws is the difficulty of their enforcement owing to the slightness or inefficiency of their sanction or of punishment for their breach.

If, when two nations are at war, one of the belligerents violates any rule of any one of the three classes, the only thing that the injured can do is to fight all the harder, and to appeal to neutrals, in the hope that then or thereafter the moral sense of the civilised world will pronounce judgment—*securus judicat orbis terrarum.*[1]

There are cases, few and far between, where something more can be done even *flagrante bello.* There are instances where reprisals can be used with effect. If open towns are bombarded, and the injured belligerent has the means, he may bombard similar towns of his enemy ; and if he does this, not by way of retaliation but after notice that if such outrages are committed he will retort, and by retorting teaches the enemy the consequence of his acts and deters him from future outrages, it seems to the writer that the act is not only warranted but even required.

So, if prisoners are ill-treated, after due warning, similar treatment may be—as has been done in this War—applied to the prisoners of the other side. But there is no use in reprisals unless you are in fact the stronger side. If you cannot bombard, at least, as many or more of the open

---

[1] The writer discussed this matter in an essay written for the Grotius Society on ' The Destruction of Merchantmen by a Belligerent,' vol. ii. of the Society's publications, pp. 175, 176.

towns of the other belligerent, if you have not prisoners, at least as many or more, you must hold your hand and suffer for the time.

There is another sanction which can be applied after war, but only by the victorious belligerent, or in cases where the belligerents are fairly equally balanced.

Stipulations may then be made as part of the conditions of peace, either for a special indemnity to be paid to the victims of outrages, or for a special trial and punishment of individuals who have offended against the laws of war, unwritten or written. Thus the United States, at the conclusion of the War of Secession, punished certain Southerners who were deemed to have ill-treated Northern prisoners.

Otherwise the sanction is only a moral one. It is not, however, without value, and gradually by the consent of nations or (as Grotius would put it) by the consent of Christian nations, certain usages limiting the extreme ferocity of war have grown up, faded away again, and then again revived, and had acquired—one would have said till recent events—an assured and certain existence for more than a century. Only a few examples need be given : that prisoners should not be tortured or sold into slavery ; that some consideration should be given to non-combatants—for instance, if they were found in a ship captured at sea they should not be left to drown, or exposed in an open boat ; or if on land, with the single exception or excuse

of hot blood during an assault, they should not
be killed or bodily injured.

These unwritten laws or customs have been
supplemented by treaty.

First, by treaties between single States, by
which in time of peace they agree together what
they will do or refrain from doing to each other
should war break out between them. The logic
of these agreements is questionable. *Ex hypothesi,*
the general Treaty of Peace and Amity between
the two States is broken, and yet certain provisions of that same treaty are to remain unbroken
—indeed, are to come into operation because of
the greater breach.

There is some parallel to this in some of the
more elaborate mercantile contracts of modern
date.[1] But in such contracts there are the
judicial tribunals to enforce such a stipulation.
There is no tribunal to judge between the warring
States. It can only be a matter of reprisals
during war, or a topic for consideration in the
terms of the succeeding Peace. Still these provisions have been not infrequent in treaties.
Some are of ancient date.

In the treaty between Great Britain and the
States General in 1667, by Art. 32, in the
event of war, enemies' merchant ships in port,
and the goods of enemies on land, are not to be
confiscated, and six months are to be allowed to
the subjects of the other nation resident in the

[1] See Zinc Corporation, Ltd. *v.* Hirsch. L.R. 1916, 1 K.B.
541, and especially p. 561.

country to transport their goods, 'whither they should think fit.'

The United States, ₊shortly after their Independence, began to introduce similar clauses into general Treaties of Commerce which they made with other nations.

By a treaty with Prussia made in 1799, which expired in 1810 but was renewed by a treaty of 1828 (Art. 23), nine months were in certain events to be allowed in case of war to the subjects of one belligerent to remove themselves and their goods; and there were further privileges of exemption from the ordinary liabilities of war for certain classes of persons.

The effect of these provisions has quite lately come into consideration. It may also be noted that there is a special provision (Art. 24) for the humane treatment of prisoners of war.

By the Treaty of Commerce of 1843, made by the United States with the Argentine Confederation (Art. 12), it seems to be provided that in case of war, citizens of either nation may remain and trade peacefully in the other country.

In a treaty of 1858 made with Bolivia, in the event of war, merchants are to have six months if at the ports, twelve months if in the interior, to arrange their affairs; and all other persons may remain in the country and keep their personal liberty and property (Art. 28).

This Article is a common form clause which had already found its way into treaties with other States in Central and South America. It appears in the following treaties : With Brazil, 1828 ; Central America, 1825 ; Chili, 1832 ; New Granada, 1846 ; Costa Rica, 1851 ; Ecuador, 1839 ; Guatemala, 1849 ; Mexico, 1831 and 1848 ; Salvador, 1850. It appears in a wider form in the treaty with Peru of 1836. Twelve months in all cases was given by the treaty with Spain of 1795 ; but that is not one of the treaties which have been renewed since the war between the two countries. These treaties may be considered as in some sense the precursors of the Convention No. 6 of the Second Peace Conference at The Hague in 1907.

A stride towards humanity was taken by the first Geneva Convention of 1864, giving neutrality and protection to ambulances and military hospitals, surgeons, bearers, chaplains, and inhabitants of the country who might bring help to the wounded, with a further provision that the wounded or sick soldiers should be entertained and taken care of, to whichever nation they might belong, and that those who were incapable by wounds of further serving should be released and sent home.[1]

Another step was the Declaration of St. Petersburg of 1868, prohibiting the use of certain explosive projectiles because of the excessive torture which wounds given by them would inflict.

There was also a Conference on the Laws of War held at Brussels in 1874 ; but no decisive conclusions were then reached. Art. 10 of the

---

[1] Further Geneva Conventions are those of 1868, principally as to maritime warfare (unratified), and 1906.

Draft Declaration then put forth could hardly have been accepted by Germany without condemnation of her action in the Franco-German War.[1]

In 1899, this matter was taken seriously in hand at The Hague, and Conventions—No. 2, concerning the laws and customs of war on land ; and No. 3, adapting the principles of the Geneva Convention to maritime warfare—were framed, and received the adherence of almost all civilised nations.[2]

Three declarations, however, were not so universally accepted.

No. 1, prohibiting for five years the discharge of projectiles and explosives from balloons ;

No. 2, prohibiting the use of projectiles containing asphyxiating or deleterious gases ; and

No. 3, prohibiting the use of expanding bullets.

Great Britain signed none of them. The United States did not sign Nos. 2 and 3. No. 1 lapsed after five years.[3]

The Second Hague Conference of 1907 proposed modifications and improvements in these

[1] The population of a non-occupied territory, who on the approach of the enemy spontaneously take up arms to resist the invading troops, without having had time to organise themselves in conformity with Art. 9, shall be considered as belligerents, if they respect the laws and customs of war.

[2] *The Hague Peace Conferences*, by A. Pearce Higgins, pp. 257, 273, *et seq*. Carnegie Endowment for International Peace, Signatures, etc., to the Conventions and Declarations of the First and Second Hague Peace Conferences.

[3] Where the Conventions of 1907 have not been ratified, it is necessary to go back upon the Conventions of 1899, which remained in force till denunciation, and therefore were in force at the outbreak of the present war.

several Conventions and added others. But though the proposed alterations were carried by votes of the majority of the States present, none of the new Conventions were universally ratified in their entirety.

Convention No. 4, concerning the laws and customs of war on land, which took the place of the former No. 2, was generally ratified except in respect of one article. Convention No. 9, concerning bombardment by naval forces in time of war; No. 10, adapting the principles of the Geneva Convention to maritime warfare, which took the place of the former No. 3; and a declaration similar to No. 1 of 1899, prohibiting ' the discharge of projectiles and explosives from balloons or by other new methods of a similar nature ' till the Third Conference met, failed to secure general ratification.[1]

It is not proposed to discuss these Conventions and Declarations in detail. Probably the experience of this War will show that improvements, and particularly further clearness and positiveness in the expressions, greater sharpness of outline should be introduced at some further Congress held for this purpose at the end of the War.

These are matters for military and naval experts, but there is a more important consideration. There is no doubt that the rules of Geneva and of The Hague have been broken in several cases. It is of no use having these rules, it is

[1] Pearce Higgins, pp. 530, 531. Carnegie Endowment, *ubi supra.*

of no use trying to improve them, unless there be some security for their enforcement. Provisions for this purpose will be suggested in Chapter IX.

So much for the laws of war as between belligerents. Now for treaties dealing with the rights and duties of belligerents in relation to neutrals.

There is a great bulk of jurisprudence on this subject to be found in Acts of State, Treaties of Commerce, and Decisions of Prize Courts. Questions on this branch of the subject arise most frequently in maritime warfare. Here the belligerent may desire to exercise three rights, any one of which will bring him into difficult relations with neutrals. The catchwords are Blockade, Contraband, and Capture of Private Property at Sea.[1]

By declaring and enforcing a blockade of an enemy's port, the belligerent invests it and prevents ingress and egress of ships and cargoes. This is an unquestioned belligerent right, and neutral States submit to it and to its enforcement by the capture and condemnation of any blockade-running vessel and her cargo.

Difficulties arise when a belligerent asserts a blockade which is not a real blockade, and thus by a side wind endeavours to effect that which he is not by the laws of war entitled to effect, a general prohibition of trade between neutrals and his

---

[1] There are consequential matters regarding the right of visit and search and as to the disputed question of protection by convoy with which it is not proposed to overload this essay.

enemy. For 'there is no more unquestionable proposition of International Law than the proposition that Neutral States are entitled to carry on upon their own account a trade with a belligerent.'[1] To proclaim therefore in a general way the blockade of a port or coast which is not invested, for the chance of catching from time to time one neutral vessel among many and condemning her for breaking the blockade, while scores of ships, perhaps belonging to other neutral States, have passed securely, is an unwarrantable act. Pushed to its extreme, it comes to declaring all the coasts of the enemy blockaded and thus prohibiting all neutral trade. And this was what was done by Napoleon with his Decrees of Berlin and Milan, and in retaliation by the British Orders in Council, both sides acting without warrant.

To provide against these illegitimate extensions, it has been common since the days of the First Armed Neutrality (1780)[2] to denounce 'paper blockades' and to stipulate that blockades shall be 'effective.'

The right of a belligerent to interfere with the trade of a neutral when it consists in carrying munitions of war to the enemy is also of ancient date and well established. Though a Neutral State since the Treaty of Washington, 1871, may be held to act unneutrally if she permits an armed body of men, or a ship of war to be

---

[1] Phillimore, *International Law*, vol. iii. sec. 161.
[2] Koch has a good passage on these subjects, vol. i. p. 463.

despatched or fitted out from her ports, her subjects have always been allowed to export munitions, subject to the penalty that if they are caught on the way they are deemed contraband and are confiscated.

Here the difficulty which arises is as to the articles to be deemed contraband. Arms and ammunition will obviously be contraband ; but many raw materials capable of being worked up either into warlike weapons or into peaceful engines of commerce, many manufactured articles available for purposes of war or of peace, articles *ancipitis usus* in the language of international lawyers, will give rise to dispute. Then there are also the cases of ' conditional contraband.' And circumstances are continually changing. Fifty years ago mineral oil, rubber, and chemicals would never have been dreamt of as being used in war. In consequence, there have been numerous treaties between States agreeing as between themselves, from time to time, what shall be deemed contraband.[1]

As to Capture of Private Property of Belligerent Nationals at sea, this also is an unquestioned belligerent right, though suggestions have been made for its abolition. Here the difficulty with neutrals arises when the ship and her cargo being, as they usually are, differently owned, one owner is an enemy and the other a neutral.

Are the two to stand and fall together—free

[1] A long list will be found in Phillimore, *International Law*, vol. iii. part 10, chap. i.

ship, free goods, enemy's ship, enemy's goods ? Or shall there be discrimination, the enemy's ship be captured and the neutral's goods go free, and *vice versâ* ?

It can be argued that there is a simplicity and convenience in the arrangement which gives to the whole adventure one national character.

If the neutral ship be seized because of carrying an enemy cargo, she is brought out of her course into a belligerent port, divested of her lading, no doubt paid a proportionate freight, but then left to find her way home. If the enemy ship be brought in, no doubt the neutral cargo is released; but it is released at a strange port, and its owner has to provide as best he can, either to sell it on the spot or forward it to its destination. Many States have adopted the rule free ships, free goods, and *vice versâ*.[1]

On the other hand, there is something arbitrary in the confiscation of the goods of a neutral which he has lawfully laden upon the ship of a nation with which his country is at peace.

But there is a deeper underlying consideration. With the doctrine of free ships, free goods, the command of the sea is of much less value. The

[1] See Phillimore, *International Law*, vol. iii. part 9, chap. x., for an enumeration of treaties providing for one rule or the other. This provision has been inserted by the United States in, it is believed, all their treaties with other American States. See *Treaties and Conventions concluded between the United States of America and other Powers since July 4, 1776*, published at Washington, 1889. The writer is indebted to the courtesy of the American Embassy in London for the opportunity of reading this book.

belligerent who has lost his merchant navy can yet provision himself and carry on his trade in neutral bottoms. Great Britain therefore steadily held to the division of the adventure until the Crimean War.

And this brings us to the Declaration of Paris. Great Britain and France were in alliance. France was guided by the other rule. She confiscated neutral cargo on enemy's ships but allowed the neutral flag to cover everything but contraband.[1] In order that the Allies might work more nearly on the same system, Great Britain waived her right of seizing enemy's property laden on board a neutral vessel unless it were contraband. She did not, however, claim to exercise the right which France claimed. She thus made an unqualified concession to neutrals. She also gave up the ancient practice of issuing letters of marque to privateers.

After the war, the Plenipotentiaries of the Seven Powers agreed to a Declaration in four articles :

1. Privateering is and remains abolished.

To this useful provision most States have formally acceded. No State has since issued letters of marque ; and the learning about privateers is happily matter of ancient history.

4. Blockades in order to be binding must be effective ;

[1] But in the Treaty of Commerce of 1786 between Great Britain and France it was provided (Art. 29) that the flag should not cover the cargo.

that is to say, maintained by a force sufficient really to prevent access to the enemy's coastline.

This article also has been generally accepted, not so much as new legislation, but as stating a principle of International Law which had at last got itself established. It has not been questioned during this War and is not likely to be disputed in future.

Arts. 2 and 3 are the controversial ones :

2. The neutral flag covers enemy's goods with the exception of contraband of war.

3. Neutral goods, with the exception of contraband of war, are not liable to capture under the enemy's flag.

By Art. 2, Great Britain abandoned her ancient claim. By Art. 3, France and other nations abandoned theirs. The unwisdom of the abandonment by Great Britain of her ancient rights was much commented on at the time.[1] It has been demonstrated during the present War.

Art. 3 is, as it happens, of no importance in this War, the German mercantile navy having been destroyed or shut up in harbour.

There has as yet been no formal abrogation or denunciation of Art. 2, though in a Declaration of March 1, 1915, put out by the British and French Governments by way of reprisal for the German Declaration of a submarine blockade, the two Governments stated that they would ' hold themselves free to detain and take into port ships carrying goods of presumed enemy

---

[1] *E.g.*, by Sir Robert Phillimore, *International Law*, vol. iii. sec. 210, and John Stuart Mill, there cited.

destination, ownership, or origin. It is not, they went on to say, ' intended to confiscate such vessels or cargoes unless they would otherwise be liable to condemnation.'

Many attempts have been made before this War to induce States to abandon the right to capture the enemy's private property at sea ; but they have not succeeded, and after the experience of the present War, it may be safely said that no such proposition would now be entertained.

The idea is one which has in times past commended itself to some philanthropists and to somewhat sentimental politicians ; but its real supporters were the statesmen of the great continental nations with large standing armies and a whole population of trained men, who wished to make all wars soldiers' wars, in which they would be certain (as they thought) of success.[1]

The writer will suggest in Chapter IX. that the Declaration of Paris be abrogated and that, if possible, the ancient rule of the prize law of Great Britain be made of universal application.

---

[1] The writer is glad to think that when the subject came up for discussion at the Conference of the International Law Association at Rouen in 1900, he and his friend, the late Lord Justice Kennedy, resolutely and successfully opposed a proposition in favour of the abolition of the right to capture private property at sea.

It has been said that it is unequal to expose private property at sea to capture when private property on land is not confiscated. But since the experience of private owners in France and Belgium at the hands of the Germans in this War, we are not likely to hear this argument again.

But he fears that, so far from this being universally accepted, there is likely to be an attack made on the principle of capture of private property at sea, an attack which the statesmen of Great Britain and France must be prepared to meet.

He has another motive for the introduction of this topic of prize law, which might appear as a digression from the main purposes of the essay, and that is the following : Germany and Austria-Hungary have, in the assertion of their belligerent rights in maritime warfare, invaded the rights of neutrals, and committed acts of inhumanity for which there is no toleration and which must be made impossible.

There is no Convention of The Hague of 1907 which deals directly with Blockade, Contraband, or the Capture of Private Property at Sea.[1]

But No. 12, relative to the establishment of an International Prize Court, does incidentally introduce these matters. By Art. 7, the proposed Court was, in the absence of treaty provisions, to apply the rules of International Law ; and Great Britain thereupon proposed a Conference with the object of reaching an agreement as to the rules of International Law which this Court would apply.[2]

The Conference met and prepared what is known as the Declaration of London of 1909.

[1] No. 13 is entitled ' Convention respecting the Rights and Duties of Neutral Powers in Maritime War ' ; but it deals with such questions as the admission of belligerent vessels and their prizes into the ports of a Neutral State.

[2] Pearce Higgins, p. 567.

It was never ratified. It contained some most questionable provisions in alteration of the recognised rules of International Law. The general object was to favour neutrals and reduce the powers of belligerents. But by an irony of fate its effect, so far as it has gone, has been disastrous to neutrals during the present War.

During the Russo-Japanese War, the Russians had sunk some English ships at sea, alleging that no harm was done as they were certain to be condemned for carrying contraband if brought into Court, and that it was dangerous or impossible to bring them into port.

There was no breach of the laws of humanity. The Russians took off and took care of the crews. But Great Britain strongly protested at the time; and before The Hague Conference of 1907, Sir Edward Grey, as Foreign Secretary, instructed the British Delegates as follows:

As regards the sinking of neutral prizes, which gave rise to so much feeling in this country during the Russo-Japanese war, Great Britain has always maintained that the right to destroy is confined to enemy vessels only, and this view is favoured by other Powers. Concerning the right to destroy captured neutral vessels, the view hitherto taken by the greater Naval Powers has been that, in the event of it being impossible to bring in a vessel for adjudication, she must be released. You should urge the maintenance of the doctrine upon this subject which British prize courts have, for at least 200 years, held to be the law.[1]

When this matter, having been postponed

[1] *The Hague Peace Conference*, Pearce Higgins, p. 624.

from The Hague Conference, came up before the Conference of London, the lame and impotent conclusion was expressed in the following articles :

DESTRUCTION OF NEUTRAL PRIZES

Art. 48. A neutral vessel which has been captured may not be destroyed by the captor ; she must be taken into such port as is proper for the determination there of all questions concerning the validity of the capture.

Art. 49. As an exception, a neutral vessel which has been captured by a belligerent warship, and which would be liable to condemnation, may be destroyed if the observance of Art. 48 would involve danger to the safety of the warship or to the success of the operations in which she is engaged at the time.

Art. 50. Before the vessel is destroyed all persons on board must be placed in safety, and all the ship's papers and other documents which the parties interested consider relevant for the purpose of deciding on the validity of the capture, must be taken on board the warship.

Art. 51. A captor who has destroyed a neutral vessel must, prior to any decision respecting the validity of the prize, establish that he only acted in the face of an exceptional necessity of the nature contemplated in Art. 49. If he fails to do this, he must compensate the parties interested and no examination shall be made of the question whether the capture was valid or not.

Art. 52. If the capture of a neutral vessel is subsequently held to be invalid, though the act of destruction has been held to have been justifiable, the captor must pay compensation to the parties interested, in place of the restitution to which they would have been entitled.

Articles 53 and 54 deal with the destruction of neutral goods.

After the clear statement of principles by the British Foreign Secretary these articles in the

Declaration of London were an act of weakness, and this war has shown the mischief of them. No door ought to be open for such outrages upon neutrals, and upon non-combatant subjects of a belligerent State when travelling on neutral vessels, as the construction put upon these articles by Germany and Austria-Hungary has enabled them to commit.

If any neutral vessel cannot be brought into port for adjudication, she should be released. The owner of neutral cargo on board an enemy ship ought equally to have a right to insist that the ship be brought into port, and that his case be tried with all the advantages which the possession of the ship's papers and knowledge of the other incidents of the voyage and the testimony of the master and crew may give him.

Still more has the neutral passenger who is entitled to travel on a belligerent merchant ship, the right to say that though he must submit to the inconveniences of the ship being brought in for condemnation, he had entered upon a lawful voyage and is entitled to be brought in the ship in to a safe port, being put to sufficient inconvenience by having had his voyage diverted and having to make his further way as best he can from the port of condemnation.

No doubt the prohibition of the practice of sinking vessels would put a stop to the German form of submarine warfare, and to some warfare by corsairs who can never hope to bring their prizes into port. But it would be much to the advantage of humanity if the old rule were restored and adhered to. The old doctrine as to capture at sea has been thought in times past to press hardly enough upon neutrals ; this Russo-German extension makes the position of neutrals almost more intolerable than that of belligerents.

CHAPTER VIII

HOW TREATIES ARE BROUGHT TO AN END

THE academical question whether Peace revives old treaties which had been dissolved by war is prudently disposed of in modern times by express provision one way or the other in the Treaty of Peace.[1]

Sometimes treaties have been made for a fixed term of years. The Treaty of Kiwerowa Hoska, 1582, between Poland and Russia was to last ten years, and was continued in 1591 for eleven years more. The Treaty of Adrianople, 1713, between Russia and Turkey, was made for twenty-five years; and the Treaty of Passarowitz between the Emperor and Turkey was to last twenty-four lunar years. An important Treaty of 1846, between the United States and New Granada concerning the Isthmus of Panama, was to last twenty years. The treaty between the United States and Prussia of 1799, which has been already referred to, expired in 1810.

It has not been unusual for Treaties of Commerce to have a time limit, or to have a provision

[1] Or by a subsequent treaty, as that of 1902 between the United States of America and Spain.

that either State has the right after a time to bring it to an end, upon notice. The exercise of this right of notice is called in diplomatic language a ' denunciation.'

Some treaties have for their sole purview future and conditional events, and only operate if and when the events happen.

In a sense this is true of all treaties of defensive alliance ; but there are special cases in which it is emphasised, as, for instance, when provision is made for assistance to the Ally if attacked by a particular Power, or in a particular portion of his territory.

The special Convention between Great Britain and Turkey at the time of the Treaty of Berlin in 1878, for the protection of the Asiatic provinces of Turkey against Russia, is a good instance.[1]

In these cases the question frequently arises whether the event is precisely within the terms of the provision ; and it is unfortunately true that States, when it has been inconvenient for them to come to the assistance of their Allies, have narrowly and closely examined their stipulations in order to see whether they must admit that what is called in diplomatic language the *casus fœderis* has arisen ; and few things are more difficult of appreciation than the justice or injustice of the refusal by a State to admit the *casus fœderis*.

An interesting example occurred when Great

[1] *Vide supra*, p. 89.

Britain, relying on the Treaty of Westminster of 1678, called upon the States General to assist her in her war with her American Colonies, France, and Spain, in 1783. The refusal of the States General to recognise this claim ended in war being declared between the two countries in the same year.

The present War has furnished two examples. At the outset Italy refused to consider that in the circumstances in which the war began she was bound by her Treaty of Triple Alliance to side with Germany and Austria-Hungary. And Greece declined to come to the assistance of Serbia when the latter State was attacked, not only by Bulgaria, in respect of which there was unquestionably a *casus fœderis*, but also by Austria-Hungary, Germany, and Turkey in alliance with Bulgaria. Whether or not the Ally be justified in refusing to recognise the *casus fœderis*, he in his turn must expect that the disappointed State will consider the treaty as at an end.

As to treaties generally, it is one of the difficulties incident to continuing stipulations, that in time one of the parties may grow weary and find the yoke too irksome to be borne, especially as the conditions of the world alter. It must be admitted that there are cases where the claim of a State to abrogate a treaty cannot reasonably be refused. That is, if she does so after giving ample notice beforehand, not retracting in the middle of an emergency or crisis, but giving such opportunity to the other State as may enable it to adapt itself to the altered condition. But the broad principle is *pactum serva.*

No State, however, can by unilateral action release itself from its obligations.

This point arose between the United States of America and France in 1798, when the United States claimed by Declaration to annul certain Conventions with France, and France insisted that the Conventions could not be thus brought to an end. When the two nations, after an interval of disturbance, concluded a fresh Treaty of Peace and Commerce on September 30, 1800, to last eight years, this particular difficulty was still undisposed of, and had to be left open, Art. 2 of the treaty being in the following terms :

> Les ministres plénipotentiaires des deux parties ne pouvant, pour le présent, s'accorder au traité d'alliance de 6 février, 1778, au traité d'amitié et de commerce de la même date, et à la convention de 14 novembre, 1788, non plus que relativement aux indemnités mutuellement dues ou reclamées, les parties, négocieront ultérieurement sur ces objets, dans un temps convenable ; et jusqu'à ce qu'elles se soient accordées sur ces points, lesdits traités et conventions n'auront point d'effet, et les relations des deux nations seront réglées, ainsi qu'il suit.

On this Koch observes :

> Pour l'intelligence de cet article il faut se rappeler que les conventions qui y sont relatées avaient été annulées par l'acte des États Unis du 7 juillet, 1798 ; mais le gouvernement français refusa avec raison de reconnaitre cet acte, parcequ'il ne depend pas d'une partie de se dégager par une simple déclaration de sa volonté d'une obligation synallagamatique. Il est de principe en droit des gens qu'un traité

entre deux puissances ne peut être rompu que par une déclaration de guerre. Cette déclaration de guerre n'avait pas eu lieu. . . .'[1]

Russia in 1871, as has been already stated,[2] had claimed to release herself from clauses of the Treaty of Paris of 1856 without the consent of the other contracting parties. But at the assembling of the Conference in London, Earl Granville made the following statement :

> The Conference has been accepted by all the consignatory Powers of the Treaty of 1856, for the purpose of examining without any foregone conclusion, and of discussing with perfect freedom, the proposals which Russia desires to make to us with regard to the revision which she asks of the stipulations of the said Treaty relative to the neutralisation of the Black Sea.
>
> This unanimity furnishes a striking proof that the Powers recognise that it is an essential principle of the law of nations that none of them can liberate itself from the engagements of a Treaty, nor modify the stipulations thereof, unless with the consent of the contracting parties by means of an amicable understanding.
>
> This important principle appears to me to meet with general acceptance, and I have the honour to propose to you, gentlemen, to sign a Protocol *ad hoc*.

The Protocol in question was then submitted to the Conference and signed by all the Plenipotentiaries.

Art. 59 of the Treaty of Berlin of 1878 appeared to provide that Batoum should be a free port. But in 1886, Russia announced that she considered this Article to be not like the other Articles, a product of general agreement, but a

[1] Vol. ii. p. 57. [2] *Vide supra*, p. 84.

spontaneous declaration of the Tsar, that the reasons for making Batoum a free port no longer existed, that its position as such was prejudicial to the well-being of the Province, and that Russia was going to terminate this position.

The British Foreign Secretary, Lord Rosebery, protested, in a despatch of July 3, against this action, but notwithstanding the protest, the Tsar, by a ukase of July 5, took away from Batoum the position of a free port.

Those who desire to free themselves from the obligations of a treaty sometimes avail themselves of a maxim of the Civil Law : *Conventio omnis intelligitur rebus sic stantibus*, which, according to the exposition of Sir Robert Phillimore, means ' when that state of things which was essential to, and the common cause of, the promise or engagement has undergone a material change, or has ceased, the foundation of the promise or engagement is gone, and their obligation has ceased.'

As he further says : ' This provision rests upon the principle that the condition of *rebus sic stantibus* is tacitly annexed to every covenant.' [1] Grotius and Vattel have devoted attention to the maxim. It is not to be applied without great caution. Grotius admits it only in cases in which it is quite clear that the existing state of things was the sole cause of the contract.[2]

[1] *Commentaries on International Law*, vol. ii. secs. 89, 90.
[2] *De jure belli et pacis*, Lib. II. c. xvi. p. 25.
Wheaton says :
Treaties expire by their own limitation, unless revived by express agreement, or when their stipulations are fulfilled by

To this limitation another condition should be annexed. The State which is about to suggest that the treaty is no longer binding should give ample notice before acting, so that other States may adapt themselves to the altered condition of things. To use diplomatic language, there must be a prior denunciation of the treaty. To act as if an existing treaty were non-existent, to abrogate it without warning, is to put the other party, who may have been relying upon it, in a worse condition than if there had been no treaty at all. The injured one has been lulled into a false security. When the crisis comes it is too late to withdraw from the contract.

But if ample notice be given beforehand, then it seems to the writer that there is a good deal to be said for the contention that the rulers of one generation cannot bind the nationals of a State in perpetuity; that with the vast changes produced by the industrial and commercial growth of the world, by new inventions and the occupation or civilisation of waste or thinly populated territories, it

the respective parties or when a total change of circumstances renders them no longer obligatory.

(*Elements of International Law*, by Henry Wheaton, LL.D., sec. cclxxv. p. 390).

Klüber says :

Les Traités cessent encore d'être obligatoires, 7" lors du changement essential de telle ou telle circonstance, dont l'existence était supposée nécessaire par les deux parties *clausula rebus sic stantibus*, soit que cette condition a été stipulé expressément soit qu'elle resulte de la nature même du Traité.

(*Droit des Gens Moderne de l'Europe*, par J. L. Klüber, 2nd ed. Paris, 1874.)

may well be that ancient stipulations have become unreasonable ; and that a State has a right to invite the other to enter into negotiations for the purpose of modifying or cancelling old relations.

Bluntschli says :

Art. 454. Le traité ne prend fin, par suite de la dénunciation d'une seule des parties contractantes, que si cela a été expressément réservé, ou si le droit de dénoncer une traité résulte des circonstances.

And in a note, he adds :

La nature du droit public exige l'admission du droit de dénoncer un traité dans certain cas, même lorsque ce droit n'a pas été réservé. Le bien des peuples peut être compromis par un traité, et une génération ne peut pas lier à perpétuité les générations subsequentes, etc.[1]

Calvo thus expresses himself both as to the power to denounce and as to the necessity of notice.

Lorsque les circonstances se sont modifiées et que les parties cessent d'être d'accord, celui des contractants dont les intérêts sont en souffrance ou qui veut définitivement rompre ses liens conventionnels est tenu de notifier à l'autre, par écrit ou verbalement, *mais d'une manière expresse*, son intention de laisser expirer le traité. Cette notification prend le nom de dénonciation. Lorsqu'elle repose sur des raisons sérieuses de convenance la dénonciation se justifie d'elle-même et ne saurait être considerée comme un procédé blessant ou injurieux pour la partie qui la reçoit.[2]

If, however, a State claim to use a treaty as if it were no treaty, but a mere ' scrap of paper ' or

[1] *Le Droit International Codifié*, p. 267.
[2] *Le Droit International*, vol. i. p. 678.

rotten parchment bond,' to break it without notice, or to act in defiance of it without even the ceremony of a notified breach, with that State unrepentant no treaties can be made, for no promises are of any avail. The only thing is for her neighbours to keep ceaseless watch and ward on their frontiers as against a barbarous tribe, and upon any outbreak to inflict such a chastisement as will at once enforce a lesson upon her and break her power to do mischief.

CHAPTER IX

THIS chapter is written on the assumption that
Great Britain and her Allies will be victorious in
the present War, not perhaps with so preponder-
ating a success as that of France over Prussia
which led to the Treaty of Tilsit in 1807, or of
the Allies over France in 1814, but still sufficient
to enable the Allies to enforce moderate and
reasonable demands. It is written on the further
assumption that the statesmen and diplomatists
of both sides will strive for a Peace which is not
an armistice nor a truce, but one as lasting as
human foresight can secure.

The War is remarkable not only as being on
the largest scale, but as involving the largest
number of powerful nations and the most con-
flicting interests which the world has known.
The matters to be determined, if not so numerous
as those determined at the Congress of Vienna
with its consequential treaties, will in combined
number and magnitude exceed those of that or
any other treaty.

First will have to be considered the settlement of claims and disputes, and, secondly, pro-

visions for preventing, wherever possible, war in future, and for making war, when it does occur, less intolerable than the present War has been.

So various are the interests that the settlement of claims and disputes must be considered State by State and nationality by nationality. Upon these subjects it is proposed to make suggestions *seriatim*.

The other half of the business of the treaty— prevention of war and improvement of the laws of war, if war there must be, will follow after the territorial and national rearrangements. But if these rearrangements are to be made with an eye to the future, it is well to consider how to eliminate provisions which would probably be useless.

This War has taught us that neutralisation of States is no good. Belgium and Luxemburg have been invaded. The Congo State has been involved in warfare. Though Greece is not at formal war, one of the Ionian Islands has been occupied by the Allies, and if Greece were in actual collision no one can suppose that the other islands would be treated as neutral.

Switzerland, it is true, has escaped, but who can say whether, if the plans of the German Staff had pointed in that direction, Switzerland might not have met with the fate of Belgium ? And with Switzerland would fall the neutralised portion of Savoy.

Buffer States have sometimes commended themselves to politicians. There has been an

idea that Alsace-Lorraine could be turned into a
Buffer State, or could be put into a similar position
with Switzerland, and made neutral, so that
there would be a chain of Buffer States—Belgium,
Luxemburg, Alsace-Lorraine, and Switzerland—
between France and Germany. But who can
doubt that if these two great nations were at war,
they would find the means of striking at each other
by land? And the experiences of Saxony at
the hands of Frederick II. are not encouraging.
The Barrier Treaties may have been helpful to
Holland; but they were injurious to the Austrian
Netherlands.

Something, it seems to the writer, is to be
hoped from the restoration of the Balance of
Power, a principle to which reference has already
been made in the first and second chapters,
and which has been in the minds of European
statesmen since the Peace of Westphalia, 1648.

The preponderance of military power which
the two great Central Empires, by reason of their
position, the size of their populations, and their
military training and preparation, possessed,
should be, and will be, reduced. In this respect,
the entry of the United States of America, with
the lead thus given to the other American States,
is invaluable. Canning's phrase is found to be
prophetic. The New World has been called in
' to redress the Balance of the Old.'

Some may say that the result of this war will
be to give to Great Britain a preponderance
and weigh down the balance in her favour to

such an extent as to make her a greater danger to the peace of the world than even the combined Central Empires. An Englishman may hope, as he will certainly pray, that she may make a just use of her strength. But the temptation which power places in the mind of mortal man, and still more so in the collective mind of aggregations of men, is too well known. The only thing to lay to our heart is the exhortation—' Be not highminded, but fear.'

Nevertheless, Great Britain's preponderance—if it results—will be of a different nature from the preponderance of the compact Central Empires. Her possessions are so scattered and, being scattered, so vulnerable from all sides, and the interests of the Dominions are so diverse, that for the purposes of offence she is, though for a different reason, as unwieldy as Russia. She has become a Confederation ; and Confederations, as has been said, seldom fight.

Before proceeding to the question of territorial and national rearrangement, we should make use of the history and historical lessons to be learnt from the previous chapters.

Inconclusive Treaties of Peace are of little value—witness Aix-la-Chapelle in 1748, the Peace of Amiens in 1802. A Peace which leaves a real claim or an earnest national aspiration unsatisfied is only a truce. The arrangements of the Congress of Vienna as to Italy and Poland ; the arrangements of 1829, 1830, and 1832, creating the Independence of Greece but drawing the line in a wholly arbitrary manner, and giving no real recognition to Greek claims; the rearrangement of Italy which left out Venetia; the Treaty of Berlin of 1878; were just as calculated to bring on war as were the Treaty of Tilsit of 1807, or the Treaty of Frankfort of 1871.

It is almost a truism that the annexation of an unwilling nationality, whether as subject to, or in forcible union with, another nationality, gains no strength from its being ratified by a treaty. The annexing nation may succeed in blending the two together. But if there be no union of hearts rupture will come at any time, soon as it did for Belgium, later for Lombardy and Venetia, later still for Norway. Or there may be constant unrest, as with the Tyrol when put under Bavaria, with North Schleswig, with Poland, and with portions, at any rate, of Alsace-Lorraine. Japan has still to win over Corea, and the United States the Philippine Islands.[1]

Cessions and retrocessions should be, if possible, absolute, not encumbered with conditions or stipulations as to the future. Protectorates may be necessary for the Turkish territories or in Africa. Otherwise they are to be avoided. Guarantees are idle things. Generally, the security for future Peace does not

---

[1] If there has to be any annexation, there is a useful clause in the Treaty of Cession of Alaska (1867) by Russia to the United States (Art. 3), which provides that the inhabitants, except uncivilised tribes, shall be made citizens of the United States, and enjoy their liberty and property and the free exercise of their religion.

lie in promises or stipulations, but in the establishment of a just and stable order.

The questions of territorial and national settlement will fall into fifteen main divisions :

1. The 'restoration of Belgium, Serbia, and Montenegro with the compensations due to them.' [1]

One form of compensation in each of these cases must be money to enable the peoples of these three States to repair the ravages of the enemy.

The amount of indemnity, for which the four allied enemies (or perhaps Turkey should be excepted) have made themselves by their actions liable, is so inconceivably large that payment in full cannot be expected ; but in the bankruptcy of our enemies, Belgium, Serbia, and Montenegro should be treated as preferential creditors, and should get something approaching to an adequate sum, not that any money can repair the wrongs done to them.

As to the compensation which takes the form of territorial advantage, it will be best to consider the cases of Serbia and Montenegro when the subject of the future condition of the Slavonic countries in Austria-Hungary comes to be dealt with. Much as Bulgaria owes to them, on account of her aggressions, it will not, it is apprehended, be right to take territory from Bulgaria to add to Serbia ; because at the end of the War of 1913, when Bulgaria was so completely beaten,

[1] Reply of the Allied Governments to President Wilson, January 10, 1917.

the lines were so drawn as to incorporate all Serb populations with Serbia and leave only Bulgars to Bulgaria.

As to Belgium, military experts may recommend some alteration of frontier for the purpose of improving her defensive power ; but otherwise it does not seem that there is any natural accretion to be made to her territory, except possibly such an annexation of the strip of Zeeland as would give Belgium one bank of the West Scheldt to the sea, or some other arrangement which would give Belgium equal rights with Holland over the West Scheldt both in war and peace.[1] This would carry with it the obligation to make to Holland, or procure for Holland, some compensation.

There is also a possible union with Luxemburg ; and this leads to the next matter to be considered in the treaty.

2. Luxemburg is entitled to her freedom from the German invader. What should be her future destiny ? Would her people prefer to remain as in times past the most vulnerable of the small States of Europe ? Or would they desire to join Germany or France ? Or would they prefer, as seems more natural, to be united to Belgium ?

It should be remembered that this nearly happened at the time of the formation of Belgium, that it was over Luxemburg that the war with Holland was prolonged and that the compromise which gave half to Belgium, and left half to the

---

[1] *Vide supra*, p. 20 and p. 52.

King of the Netherlands as Grand Duke, was a mere concession to dynastic claims.

3. As to Roumania, France, and Russia, there must be, to start with, a restoration to the *status quo ante bellum.*[1] The territories occupied by the Austrians and Germans must be evacuated by them forthwith, if they have not already been driven out.

4. Japan's first contribution to the War has been her ejection, with the co-operation of Great Britain, of the Germans from China. It is to be supposed that the Germans will not be restored to the territory from which they have been ejected, or permitted any military occupation of any part of China whether under a lease or otherwise.

Probably Japan will join with Australia and New Zealand in the desire that no foothold is left to Germany in the Pacific.

5. Portugal has her boundary questions to settle in East Africa.

6. France will desire to have her lost departments.[2]

Here, it seems to the writer that some care will have to be taken to consult the feelings of the inhabitants of Alsace and of those of Lorraine. It may be, one cannot yet tell, that there are

[1] The evacuation of the invaded territories in France, in Russia, in Roumania, with just reparation. (Reply to President Wilson.)

[2] The restitution of provinces formerly torn from the Allies by force against the wish of their inhabitants. (Reply to President Wilson.)

districts in which the inhabitants have become German in sentiment, and their young men, having fought on the side of Germany, feel that she is their nation.

If this be so, one would regret it. One would desire France to have back all that was taken from her and that she has so patiently striven to recover. But it would be unjust and it would be dangerous to transfer populations against their will. The unhealed sore of 1871 would be replaced by the unhealable sore of 1917 or 1918.

When the line comes to be drawn there is a consideration not to be neglected. The boundary, whether it throws a few villages, whose inhabitants could be removed or compensated, to one side or the other, ought to be drawn so as to give a strategically strong defence, to both sides if possible, anyhow, to France.

The writer has already referred to Sir Thomas Holdich's work on Political Frontiers and Boundary-making.

France would seem to have the next claim to the benefit of the pecuniary indemnities to be paid. Indeed, in her case the Germans seem to be industriously increasing day by day the damages which they ought ultimately to discharge.

7 and 8. ' The liberation of the Italians as also of the . . . Roumanians from foreign domination ' is also one of the aims of the Allies.[1]

The cases of Italy and Roumania are closely

---

[1] Reply to President Wilson.

alike, except that Italy has had no serious occupation of her territories and might therefore take her sole compensation in the form of ' the redress of the grievances ' (to use Professor Bernard's words) for which she went to war ; while Roumania would naturally expect a share in the pecuniary indemnity in addition to the redress of her grievances. Both States went to war because there were people of their nation and tongue outside their limits, suffering under an alien yoke, desiring and desired to be united with them. In both cases the difficulty will lie in drawing the line of demarcation.

Italy may prefer a fair claim to the Trentino, a territory originally subject to a Prince Bishop, forming part, it is true; of the Austrian Circle in the German lands of the Empire, but chosen because it was in Italy and not in Germany, as the seat of the famous Council[1] and inhabited, as it is believed, by an Italian and Italian-speaking people. But towards Görz, Carniola, and Istria, while some territory is certainly Italian and the people in it would desire (which is the important thing) to form part of the Kingdom of Italy, it is, except for an

---

[1] Sarpi, *Istoria del Concilio Tridentino*, Mendrisio, 1835. Lib. I. cap. lxviii. The Bishop of Trent was under the Patriarch of Aquileia, and in this Italian province and not in the Austrian province of Salzburg. (Sprüner, *Historisch Atlas Deutschland*, No. 13 ; Italien, No. 6.) But its Bishop signed the Recess of Augsburg, 1555 ; and the bishopric appears on the Matricula of the Empire (Schmauss, *Corpus Juris Publici S.R. Imperii*, ed. 1774, pp. 89, 205, 1028, 1332, 1420).

expert, difficult to say where the Italian should
end and where the Slav should begin.

If indeed the choice is between an Austro-
Hungarian dominance or Italian freedom, no
humane person would hesitate. But if there were
to be a South Slavonic Confederacy, there would be
a debatable land of some extent, through which it
will be difficult to draw the line of demarcation
with fairness to both nationalities.

The claim of Roumania to the Roumanian
and Roumanian-speaking portion of Transylvania
and Bukovina is equally good up to a point and
equally hard to delimit. In both cases, that of
Italy and that of Roumania, a good defensive
frontier is one of the objects to be attained.
Italy has felt this need on the side of the Isonzo
during the present War.

9. Russia will (as the Allies have intimated)
demand evacuation of her invaded territories
with compensation.

Poland and the territory claimed by Roumania,
separate Russia from Germany and Austria-
Hungary. Her territorial compensation, therefore,
if she is to have territorial compensation, and it
may be that she does not now desire any, will
come out of the Turkish dominions; and the
case of Turkey will be handled later.

10. Great Britain will have made in proportion to her population as large a sacrifice of life
as any of the Allies. Of her wealth she will
have given out of proportion, and so vastly

that Germany and her Allies could never make it good.

At the outset of the war she had ' no grievance to redress.' She took up arms to stop aggression.

In the general settlement her main compensation will lie in the assurance of future peace. But her Colonies and India will have to be considered. In Europe she seems to have only two needs—one is quite a small one. If she keeps Cyprus she will no longer pay tribute for it, either to the Porte or to any other ruler of Constantinople.

The other matter is Heligoland, which she took from the Danes during the Napoleonic Wars, kept at the Congress of Vienna, and transferred to Germany as a make-weight in the arrangements as to East Africa in 1890. So dangerous a sea fortress cannot be left in Germany's keeping. But it would be too much to expect that we should keep it at the doors of Hamburg. Moreover, it would always afford a temptation to a *coup de main*. The writer would suggest that it be dismantled, restored to its pristine conditions of a bathing-place and rabbit-warren, and thus handed over to its original possessor, Denmark. As a fortress it would be a *damnosa hereditas*, for it would, as has been said, tempt a *coup de main*. But if it were an open island and Germany seized it, she could be forced to restore it before she could fortify it.

If Denmark, as a reward for accepting this

deposit, were to receive the accession of the Danish-speaking portion of Schleswig, as was proposed at the Treaty of Prague, justice would be done to a nationality whose deputies have never ceased to protest in the Reichstag against the annexation, and it would be a step towards ' the reorganization of Europe . . . based on respect for nationalities.' [1]

11. The future of the German Colonies will probably form one of the most difficult subjects of negotiation.

The Colonies in the Pacific have been captured by Australia and New Zealand. They are their peculiar prizes, and history teaches us how susceptible is a colony if the Mother Country gives up what the colony has won. Our North American colonists are said never to have forgiven Great Britain for the surrender of Cape Breton at the Peace of Aix-la-Chapelle in 1748, after they had been at such pains to take the great fortress of Louisburg; and it has been surmised that the ill-feeling then engendered was a cause of the War of Independence. Japan also, as has been already observed, will probably not desire German stations in the Pacific.

So to the German colonies in the Pacific the rule *uti possidetis* is likely to be applied. They will remain in the hands of their conquerors, who, it is to be trusted, will administer them at

---

[1] Reply to President Wilson.

least as well and as satisfactorily to the natives as their former German masters.

The same considerations will prevent the retrocession of South-West Africa. There are in addition the strongest motives of humanity. For it was here that the Germans in power gave such proofs of their cruelty to the natives in time of peace, and of their ferocity and un-scrupulousness to the natives and to the Cape troops during the war.

As to East Africa, the Cape people seem to make the same demand. From this part of the world, as also from West Africa, there comes a consensus of opinion (at least as it reaches British ears) of all those who have to do with the natives, that the Germans are bad and cruel adminis-trators and likely, if they were allowed to re-turn, to take terrible vengeance upon those of the native population who have adhered to the British or French.

If any colony or part of a colony, whether in East Africa, the Cameroons, or Togoland, is to be restored to them, special provisions of a temporary character must be taken to protect the natives.

It will not be enough to have the usual Clause, referred to by Lord Palmerston in 1856, that ' When a year is terminated in the course of which the armies of one country have occupied the territory of another, it is the invariable practice that there shall be an agreement between the parties to insure a complete amnesty to all subjects of either Power, who may have been at all committed in the progress of hostilities.'[1] There must be some further protection for the natives. The administration might be kept for a while in British or French hands. The province might be in depôt for some years.

But it may be that the Allies will not trust Germany with any power over subject races. In that case France and Great Britain would divide her colonies, except so far as the claims of Portugal come in.[2]

12. Poland. The late Tsar intimated his intention to restore the Kingdom of Poland with an independent administration; and the Russian Provisional Government, on March 30, 1917, stated that the Russian nation 'recognises also the absolute right of the brother nation of Poland to decide its own lot by the exercise of its own will,' and ' regards the creation of an independent Polish State formed of all the territories of which the majority of the population is Polish, as a pledge of a durable peace in the remodelled Europe of the future.' The Allies are reported as having accepted and endorsed this statement in a document put forth at Paris on April 15, 1917.

It will be observed that Polish does not include Lithuanian or Ruthene. Whether the effect of this declaration would be to extend Poland, so far as Russia is concerned, beyond the Kingdom of Poland established by the Congress of Vienna does not appear. Probably it would not.

[1] Quoted in Phillimore's *International Law*, vol. iii. sec. 511, note. *Vide supra*, p. 8 ; Chapter VI. p. 105.

[2] *Vide supra*, p. 148.

But the manifesto points to a Poland made up also of Prussian and Austrian Polish Provinces. West Prussia—an ancient part of Poland, but said to be German-speaking, a province necessary to the continuity of Prussia and assigned to Prussia at the First Partition of 1772—could not with reason be taken from Germany. But all principles of nationality would require that the Polish-speaking Provinces, whose deputies have constantly protested in the Reichstag against their absorption, should be allowed the oppor- tunity of forming part of the new Poland.

As to Austrian Poland, about half is Ruthenian or Ukrainian, and may prefer to remain with Austria, if it is not joined to the other Ruthenes in Russia. Cracow and the western half is Polish ; but the Poles in Austria have lately fared well ; and few could tell beforehand which connection the people of this part of Galicia would prefer.

13. As to the Slavonic and Roumanian lands in Austria-Hungary. The reply of the Allies to President Wilson speaks of ' the liberation . . . of the Slavs, Roumanians, and Czecho-Slovaks from foreign domination.'

The carelessness of expression in this sentence has been the subject of comment. The Czecho- Slovaks are not distinct from the Slavs. They are Slavs. Perhaps by *Slavs* was meant the Southern Slavs of Carinthia, Carniola, Croatia, Istria, Dalmatia, and Bosnia Herzegovina.

As to the wishes of the Czecho-Slovaks in Bohemia and Moravia we know little. It may be that the Censorship has prevented news from reaching us. There have been stories of insurrection in Bohemia and wholesale desertion of Bohemian soldiers ; and a distinguished exile, Professor Masaryk, expresses in *The New Europe* what he conceives to be the desire of his fellow-countrymen, either for complete independence or, at any rate, legislative autonomy. But we do not know whether his view is largely shared.

In the map published with Vol. II., No. 15, of *The New Europe* the distribution of the two races, Czechs and Slovaks, is drawn by a hand not unfavourable to their race claims. Even so, the map leaves a large part of Bohemia wholly German ; and the census makes one-third German and two-thirds of the two other races.

As to the South Slavonic States, we know what strong measures Austria had to use to subjugate Bosnia Herzegovina, and how frightened Austria-Hungary has been of a Southern Slav Confederation forming round Serbia as a nucleus. The Agram treason trials and her demands upon Serbia after the assassination of the Archduke and Duchess also show this.

If the pressure can be removed and we can get at the real feeling of these peoples, it may be that we shall find them demanding a Confederacy of all the Slav nations within the Austro-Hungarian dominions (except Ruthenians and Poles), with Serbia and Montenegro joined, or two Confederations, one in the north and one in the south ; and if so, it would be not only right but politic to

12

support them. Confederations are peace-loving (as has been said) and form an element of stability ; and within a Confederation there may be quite small as well as larger States. But to interfere merely for the sake of weakening Austria-Hungary would be wrong.

14. Suggestions have been thrown out that in order to destroy the aggressive power of Germany her Empire should be forcibly dissolved.

The writer would protest with all his might against this. The union of the German nation has been the result of the thought, toil and self-sacrifice of her finest spirits for generations. Its dissolution would be the reverse of that ' respect for nationalities ' of which the Allies speak. It would create a lasting sore, a perpetual unrest, and would be a defiance of all the teachings of history which it has been the object of this essay to concentrate and focus.

Even if it be true that Austria-Hungary will remain so closely connected with Germany as to make the two Powers almost one, or that, at any rate, if the Slavs break away, the German remnant, with the Magyars, will perforce agglomerate themselves to Germany, still it should not be done. Indeed, in the latter case a strong Slav State would materially assist in preserving the Balance of Power.

The satisfaction of the various claims upon her may take away from Germany North Schleswig, Alsace-Lorraine, and Prussian Poland. Germany

Proper should be allowed to remain one nation and State if she so desires.[1]

15. Turkey. The writer hardly dares to submit any suggestion for dealing with the graver matters concerning the Turkish Empire. A few words may be said.

It is presumed that the independence of the Sultans of Egypt and Mecca will be recognised, that Albania will be practically independent, that in whosesoever hands Constantinople remains, the right of free and unfettered commercial passage through the two Straits and Sea of Marmora, from and to the ports of the Black Sea and Sea of Azov, will be established on the broadest lines and the firmest footing.

The Straits and the two Seas find their nearest parallel in the St. Lawrence and the Great Lakes. The rule of the Congress of Vienna as to rivers (which has been applied to the St. Lawrence), securing freedom of passage to the upper riparian proprietors, should be applied from the Upper Danube onward, as well as from the Don and Volga, to the mouth of the Dardanelles.

The reply of the Allies to President Wilson puts forward as one of their objects ' the setting free of the populations subject to the bloody tyranny of the Turks and the turning out of Europe of the Ottoman Empire as decidedly foreign to Western civilisation.'

---

[1] It is barely possible that the German elements in Austria might combine with Bavaria to form a separate South Germany.

That every humane person would desire that all populations should be freed from the rule of the official or governing Turk, that every Christian would desire that Constantinople should once again be a Christian city, that if Russia desired to have Constantinople Great Britain need have no fear, are propositions which the writer has supported any time during the last forty years.

But it does not appear from the recent manifesto of the Provisional Russian Government as if Constantinople were now desired; while to Roumania and the States higher up the Danube, to Bulgaria, and to the State—whatever it may be —to which the Asiatic shores of the Black Sea belong, it may be a matter of great importance that some other arrangement should be made for the custody of their outlet into the Mediterranean.

Lastly, if the Ottoman Empire be turned· out of Europe, whither is it to be turned? Since the Treaty of Berlin it has been the Asiatic subjects of the Porte, especially the Armenians, that have been treated the worst. They have been the chief victims of its ' bloody tyranny.'

In this state of uncertainty and difficulty, it is possible to make tentative suggestions :

1. With regard to the conquests of Great Britain and Russia the rule *uti possidetis* could be applied, so that each could retain her conquests.

2. France may desire to reassert her old interest in the nature of a Protectorate of the tribes in the Lebanon.

3. There is still Italy's possession of some of the Islands, which are inhabited by Greeks though not as yet part of Greece, to be considered.

4. Constantinople and the shores of the Straits and Sea of Marmora might be placed under the dominion of a small protected State.

5. The remnant of the Turkish Empire could be invited to form a new State under the control of the four Powers above mentioned.

6. Anyhow, care should be taken that Turkey does not remain under German influence, and that there is not a German dominion from Berlin to Bagdad.

So far the writer has endeavoured to follow the Reply of the Allies as a guide to future national and territorial arrangements, whether they be by way of compensation to the victors or by way of redress of grievances.

In addition, there will be the usual 'Clauses of Amnesty' (to return to Professor Bernard's phraseology). These, it is presumed, will be for the ordinary soldier and citizen in the widest form which diplomatic precedent suggests.

All inhabitants of territories retroceded by the Allies will be protected. Scrupulous care will be taken that all prisoners of war be released.

The excuse may be made by Germany that some are detained for common law crimes. If any such answer be made it should not be accepted without investigation, and delivery should be insisted on, unless the alleged crime be serious and the proof that it was committed, clear. In the same way the Allies will release their ordinary prisoners. But there will be enemies with whom a further reckoning will be necessary.

If the time has not come, it will soon come, when war will be recognised as such a calamity, and in nine cases out of ten, such an unnecessary calamity, that not only should the aggressor State, and with the State all its citizens collectively, suffer, but the rulers or statesmen who have caused or induced their nation to enter into war should pay in person.

Napoleon was so made to pay when he was sent to St. Helena. He was kept captive not as a prisoner of war, for his country was at peace; not as an ordinary criminal, for he had committed no crime against the law of France; nor because he had been guilty of ' War crime ' (to use the modern phrase). He was kept captive because he had been a wanton disturber of the peace of Europe. He had had his lesson in 1814, when he was reduced to the Sovereignty of the Isle of Elba. In 1815 he was punished. It is a fate which may overtake other sovereigns, presidents, and ministers.

But if the Allies do not insist upon any such retribution for the wanton disturbance of the Peace of the whole world, there are war crimes for which punishment should be exacted, such punishment as will render the present criminals incapable of further crime and deter others in the future.

The writer trusts that it will be a term of the

Peace that there be a strict investigation into some of the worst of the many war crimes committed by Germans, and he fears he must add, Austrians.

The man, or men, really responsible who gave the order *en connaissance de cause* should be discovered, he or they should be called upon to make their defence before a Court Martial, and if found guilty be punished with death, or such less sentence as the Court may award.

Some of these men will be subordinate officers. At least it is to be hoped that some of the atrocities committed will have had no higher sanction. In other cases, when the subordinate has been acting under higher authority, his plea that he obeyed orders may for this occasion be accepted.[1] Then he who gave the order must pay the penalty, whether he be General or Admiral in command, Minister, or Sovereign.

Grotius, the main object of whose work, ' On the Laws of War and Peace,' was to prevent cruelty and lessen severity in war, when he comes to deal with the right of the conqueror over his prisoners, after pointing out that a distinction may be drawn unfavourably against those who were the authors of the war, proceeds :

' No mercy is sometimes shown to those who are taken prisoners or have surrendered, or their surrender ' on the condition that their lives should be spared is not accepted, if they have continued in arms notwithstanding that they

---

[1] *Vide infra* as to provision making this plea inadmissible in future.

knew the war to be an unjust one . . . or if they have broken faith or any other rule of the law of nations . . .'[1]

This is a wholesome doctrine and necessary for these times.

The enemy States will have to submit to the occupation of sufficient of their territory to guarantee the payment of the indemnity and the performance of any other temporary conditions imposed upon them.

The remaining subjects of the treaty are those in which the United States of America and. the other American States (who, as these pages are being written, seem following her example), and China, will take the greatest interest, and in respect of which their presence at the Congress will be, as Mr. Lloyd George has pointed out, especially desirable.

They must, to a certain extent, be treated together. And yet this seems paradoxical, for one subject is the prevention of future war, and the other contemplates future war and seeks to regulate it. But in reality there is a close connection between them, for to deprive a State of the power of truculence or of ' frightfulness,' to use the accepted translation of the German *schrecklichkeit*, may be to deter it from going to war. Among the provisions for the future, there-

---

[1] Interdum in captos aut deditos saevitum aut deditionem sub vitae pacto non acceptam si qui de injustitia belli convicti tamen in armis perstitissent . . . si fidem violassent aut aliud gentium jus. . . . *De Jure Belli et Pacis*, Lib. III. cap. xi. secs. 5 and 16. See also cap. vii.

fore, one will be the amendment and enforcement of the laws of war.

A general outline of these laws has been given in Chapter VII. Many of them go into technical details as to which it would be unwise for one who is neither a naval nor a military expert to write.

The suggestions, which the writer proposes to make, run on broader lines.

First of all, as to amendment. This may take the form of new legislation, that is an addition to existing rules, or it may take the form of declaration asserting the existence of rules, though they have been obscured and neglected.

The following points require to be made good in one way or the other : Decent treatment of non-combatants. There should be prohibition of the practice stated to have been used by the Germans in Belgium and elsewhere, of sending unarmed men and women and children of the country in front of their forces as a screen against the enemy's fire.

There is a story of calculated brutality and horror inflicted upon the women of Liège as an example of what Germany, when thwarted, might do, which, if it be true, should lead to the trial of the offenders or offender, and which, even if if be not true, has been so much reported that it would be desirable to state that such a practice was contrary to the laws of war.

The enslaving of men and women, which has been practised by the Germans in Northern France and Belgium and by Bulgaria in Serbia, and is said to be threatened by Austria in Roumania, must be declared unlawful. It is perhaps hopeless to forbid vulgar loot or the carrying away or destruction of artistic treasures and monuments. In every settlement after a war, those who do these things have in the end to pay for them.

At sea, it must be made an offence against the laws of war—a war crime—to sink merchant vessels which are not seeking to escape and which have not been summoned to surrender ; and equally a crime, when they have surrendered, to put those on board into open boats out of sight of land, or in rough weather. Belligerents who do this might almost as well imitate the ancient pirates and make men walk the plank.

It must also be made an offence against the rights of neutrals according to International Law, to destroy any neutral vessel in any circumstances; except when she is seeking to avoid capture. Also it must be made an offence against the rights of neutrals to destroy even a merchant vessel of a belligerent without providing for the safety of any neutral passenger on board.

This provision may seem to be only a repetition of the provision making it a war crime to sink merchantmen of the belligerent without providing for the crew ; but it gives the neutral State a further right, and the protection to the neutral might be more ample.

The next class of provisions should be : Any order to commit any war crime by land or sea— that is, all acts forbidden by the Conventions of

Geneva and St. Petersburg, and those of The Hague, which are generally accepted and enforced, and the war crimes to be set forth in the new treaty —should be declared to be unlawful orders which cannot be given by the superior officer, and which, if given, no soldier or sailor is bound to obey, so that he cannot plead obedience to orders as his justification.

Under the old rules of war no spy could plead that he was acting under orders; no soldier who first showed the flag of truce or held up his hands and then fired upon those who came to receive his surrender, could plead that he was acting under the orders of his captain. Both captain and soldier would be shot or bayoneted without mercy. Such orders are no orders; and this doctrine should be extended to all other war crimes.

The next step is to provide for an enforcement of these rules. Whether they be laws of war as between belligerents, or rules of International Law as between a belligerent and a neutral, the difficulty of providing a sanction is the difficulty which confronts every student of International Law. But the writer thinks that in this case he sees his way to suggest some sanction.

His proposals are as follows :· The form of the treaty should be such that each State, party to it, contracts with each and every other State which is a party, that in the event of war between it and any other State, parties to the treaty, it will observe towards the State with which it is at war, all the agreed rules of the laws of war ; and that any other State, party to the treaty, may deem it an offence against itself that the contracting State has violated the laws of war, each such violation, though not a direct injury to the neutral State, being considered nevertheless as an indirect injury, by reason of the lowering of the standard of conduct.

It would be further provided that the neutral State should have a *locus standi* to remonstrate, and if its remonstrance were unheeded, to proceed to acts of retorsion,[1] *voies de fait*, such as an em· bargo on the persons, ships, and property of subjects of the treaty-breaking nation, and in the extreme case, war.

In this way it would be made clear that any breach by a belligerent is not merely a breach of contract with the other belligerent or belligerents, but is a breach of contract with every State, neutral as well as belligerent, which is a party to the International Convention.

The reason of the thing points to this. Every violation of the laws of war, every breach of the dictates of humanity is injurious to nations not engaged in the war, as well as to nations which are engaged. It establishes a precedent which can, and probably will, be used in future wars—in wars in which some of these States now neutral may hereafter be engaged. It is to the interest of the civilised world that these provisions should be upheld ; and every State which is a party to the

[1] Phillimore, *International Law*, vol. iii. secs. 7, 8, and 25.

Convention should be recognised as injured by its breach ; and the treaty-breaker should know that the breaches may be redressed not only by reprisals on the part of the other belligerents, but by some action on the part of any or all of the neutral States.

Secondly, in respect of the conduct of belligerents towards neutrals. A determined effort will no doubt be made at the Congress to abolish the capture of private property at sea, except in the case of contraband, and probably to limit articles of contraband.

The writer has already expressed,[1] but must again repeat, his earnest hope that this effort will not prevail. He is conscious that his opinion is influenced by the fact that the retention of the rule is for the interest of Great Britain ; but he believes that the retention is also for the peace of the world. Destruction or capture of private property on land there has been and always will be. It is iale to treat war as a mere duel between the armed forces of the belligerents. But the nearer the approach to this idea of duel, the more the encouragement of great standing armies [and navies], the severer becomes the competition in time of peace, till economic exhaustion supervenes, or till one or other of the contending nations determines to bring the strife to an issue by war.

A valuable remedy against the disease of great armaments is provided when war is made a contest between the belligerent nations in their

[1] *Vide supra*, p. 126.

entirety, States and citizens all alike being concerned and being as vulnerable on their commercial and industrial as on their military sides. So far from allowing the rule to be abolished, it must be brought back to its former strictness.

The Declaration of Paris gives a double advantage to the belligerent who is inferior in sea power. Under the old French rule he had an advantage, inasmuch as if his ships were all destroyed he could still convey his goods in neutral bottoms; but his ships as vehicles of neutral commerce became unpopular, as the belligerent flag rendered the neutral cargo liable to capture.

Under the English rule belligerent property, whether ship or cargo, was captured, neutral property of either kind went free.

The Declaration of Paris allowed the belligerent to offer his ships as safe vehicles for neutral commerce (thereby departing from the French rule), and to have his goods' safely carried under a neutral flag (thereby departing from the English rule). It would be better to have the French rule than nothing. But the English rule is the logical and the really effective rule.

Blockade is admitted on all hands as a legitimate act of warfare; but blockade or investment of a garrisoned town by land forces derives its chief value from the distress which it imposes upon the entire population, civil as well as military.

On the other hand, while contending for the preservation of the present law of maritime capture and for a return to its original strictness, the Allies must equally insist upon the suppression of those practices which, first introduced during the Russo-Japanese War, have attained their hideous and inhuman development at the hands of Germany and Austria-Hungary in the present War.

The rule of law must be declared in the sense already stated in Chapter VII. of this essay,[1] and should then, like other rules of law respecting the conduct of belligerents towards neutrals, receive all the sanction that can be obtained for it.

For this purpose a similar arrangement to that already suggested for enforcing the laws of war between belligerents should obtain. Each State, party to the treaty, should contract with every other State, party to the treaty, that in the event of war between it and any State, party to the treaty or not, it would observe not only to this neutral State, but to all other neutral States parties to the treaty, the rules of International Law —both those generally recognised and those particularly established by the treaty—and a *locus standi* and right of retorsion should be given on the same grounds to each State party to the treaty.

These provisions might develop into a code of universal application, if provision were made, as has been made in the case of the Geneva and Hague Conventions, for other States not parties to the treaty adhering to it, taking its benefits and undertaking its obligations.

[1] *Vide supra*, p. 126.

No doubt there are objections to these proposals. It may be said that they encourage intermeddling, and may be used by some powerful and ambitious State to further its ends. But, on the other hand, if neutrals had been given a legal right to interpose either on behalf of humanity in respect of infringements of the laws of war, or on behalf of weaker neutrals against whom there had been an undue exercise of belligerent rights, their interposition at some early stage in the war, before matters had been embittered as they have been, might have been most effective.

History tells us of some instances of attempts to remedy lack of solidarity among neutrals. Both the Treaties of Armed Neutrality were attempts in this direction.

One side of the Monroe Doctrine, in the view taken of it by modern American statesmen, is that it is a claim by the most powerful State of the American Continent to treat an aggression upon any other State of that continent as an injury to itself. In this view there would be a Monroe Doctrine for all the States party to the treaty.

Lastly, for any securities which can be invented to prevent or at least postpone future war.

Limitation of armaments is a seductive proposal. The writer wishes that he had ever found it worked out in a practical form. It is hardly possible that any State would altogether give up having an army. It is certain that most States would refuse (reasonably or unreasonably it is unnecessary to decide) to dispense with one.

If there is to be an army what is to be the limit ? A fixed number for each State ? Those which are compact would have a vast advantage. Compare the position of Austria-Hungary with that of Russia, or that of a State which has few or no foreign possessions with that of France, Great Britain, or the United States. A percentage of the population ? This gives too much to the more populous nations. Moreover these limitations can all be evaded, as was done by Prussia after 1807, by passing the manhood of the nation in turn through the army, or by giving military training to the police.

It might be possible to have an agreement of States as to the period of military training if there was universal conscription. The writer confesses that for purposes of discipline he would wish all the young men of every nation to pass for twelve months into the ranks of the army or navy. His regret is that some corresponding discipline cannot be invented for young women. But it would be necessary to fix an international period for this training.

In the case of the Navy proportionate reduction is even more difficult. The extent of coast to be protected, the dispersion of the national territory over the world, the amount of commerce, varies for each State.

Arbitration is the other remedy. How much good arbitration has done can be read in Dr.

13

Darby's most useful work.[1] At present it is an admirable remedy when States have a disputed point but do not want to fight. It is of no value when they want to fight. In the first case they are like people who do not want to go to law but must somehow get some matter between them settled. In the second case they are like people who have quarrelled and are only too glad of any pretext for going to law.

Can reference to some disinterested body be made generally useful ? The writer thinks so upon the following terms : First, it must be applicable to all cases. There must be no exception of cases of national honour and so forth. Every dispute must be referred in some form to a disinterested tribunal before the State goes to war.

Against this it will be said that there are some claims to which no State could submit ; there are cases where, if the claim were submitted to arbitration and the award was one way, no State could obey the award. The writer entirely agrees.

There are rights with which no State will part except under the compulsion of defeat in war. No award of arbitration ordering Serbia to do what Austria-Hungary exacted of her would have been obeyed by Serbia. No threat of war would in times past have induced Great Britain to give up her asylum for political refugees.

But short of arbitration, mediation, or the submission of the question to a Tribunal of Advice, Opinion, or Conciliation would often save war. It

[1] *International Tribunals,* by W. Evans Darby, LL.D., 1904.

would give time to think, for passion to cool, and for a way out to be found without loss of dignity.

The provisions as to mediation recommended by the Congress of Paris in 1856[1] should be modified and extended, and submission to it or to arbitration made compulsory.

To compare very small things with great, the writer believes that in France and other nations which have taken the French codes for their model, ordinary disputes as to breaches of contract or debt not involving large matters are or may be submitted in the first instance to the *Juge de Paix*. He pronounces an opinion which is in form a decision, but is in substance only an expression of his view, and as such a guide to the parties, being the opinion of a disinterested person of some training and status. Neither party is bound by it. Either may go to law afterwards. But they have both had to pause, listen, and reflect. So would the writer have it, when disputing States were not willing to go to a formal arbitration or to undertake to submit to an award which might be adverse.

Second point. If in ordinary civil life the contract contain an arbitration clause, a 'submission to arbitration,' as English lawyers phrase it, exists, and either party can compel arbitration. He notifies the other party of his claim, puts it in his own way, nominates his arbitrator. If the other party do not nominate, the one arbitrator decides and the Courts compel obedience. If

[1] *Vide supra*, p. 85.

the other party come into the arbitration, the arbitrators decide whether the claim is one which arises under the contract and whether it is good or bad.

But International Arbitration Treaties hitherto have only been agreements to agree. Neither party State can take the other before the Tribunal of The Hague or before any other tribunal, or insist upon any arbitration at all.

The general promise to arbitrate is of itself of little value. It only imposes the moral duty on the two States to try and agree upon the question to be decided and the tribunal and the mode of arbitration. Lawyers and statesmen know that the statement of the question to be decided is usually the most controversial matter. Each arbitration in Dr. Darby's book has been the result of a Convention *ad hoc*.

The Constitution of the United States happens to throw this into a very clear light. Every treaty requires the sanction of the Senate. It was attempted to make Arbitration Treaties according to which the subsequent Convention submitting any matter in dispute which arose to arbitration in accordance with promise should be an act of the Executive only. The Senate refused to agree to this. It said that each Convention is a treaty, none the less a treaty because it is made in compliance with a previous treaty. Each separate Convention as it arises must have a sanction.

To meet this difficulty it should be provided

that there be standing Tribunals, whether of Arbitration, Conciliation, Mediation, or Advice, which any State may invoke as of right.

Third point. The scheme already suggested when improvement of the laws of war was under consideration must be applied also to this matter. Every State party to the great treaty must contract with every other State party to the treaty that it will observe these provisions, so that the making of war without a previous reference to the disinterested Tribunal would be a breach of contract with, and an offence against, every State party to the treaty, and might be lawfully resented and repressed by all or any of them.

With the immediate causes of war taken away by a just distribution of territory and recognition of the claims of nationality, and with these precautions for the future superadded, we may reasonably hope for a general and lasting peace. It may be said that the precautions are ineffective instruments. They only interpose obstacles and delays. It is true ; but nations, like individuals, are swept away for the moment by gusts of passion.

Time to think, to learn the truth, to listen to the voice of a friend will prevent the outbreak of many a strife.

If the United States had waited little more than one mail they would have learnt that Great Britain had made a step towards redressing their grievance, and probably there would have been no War of 1812.

With equal probability we may say that if the British public had given itself time to learn the true sequence of dates, it would have recognised in the destruction of the Turkish Fleet at Sinope a legitimate act of warfare and not a piece of pre-war treachery by Russia, and there would have been no Crimean War of 1854, and that if Bismarck had given time to Germany and to France to learn the truth about the Benedetti incident, there would have been no Franco-German War in 1870.

Not for many generations will the horrors and miseries of this war be forgotten.

In hot blood anything may be done. Designing rulers may pervert their peoples. An angry people will overcome the counsels of the wisest ruler. But we may believe and hope that after this experience the nations of the earth will not in cold blood put their hands to such another war.

CHRONOLOGICAL LIST
OF TREATIES

TO WHICH REFERENCE IS MADE IN
THE TEXT

Poland and Russia . .	(Kiwerowa Hoska)	1582
France and Turkey . .	(Capitulations) .	1604
Spain and the States General	. . . .	1648
France and the Empire .	(Münster) } West-	1648
The Empire and Sweden .	(Osnabrück) } phalia	
France and Spain . .	(Pyrenees) . .	1659
The Empire, Sweden, Poland	(Oliva). . .	1660
and Prussia		
Poland and Russia . .	(Andrusovo) .	1667
England and the States General	. . . .	1667
France and Spain . .	(Aix-la-Chapelle) .	1668
England and Turkey . .	(Capitulations) .	1675
The Emperor, Spain, England,	(Nimeguen) . .	1678
States General, Sweden and		
France		
England and the States General	(Westminster) .	1678
Russia and Poland . .	(Moscow) . .	1686
France, Great Britain, States	(Ryswick) . .	1697
General, Spain and the		
Empire		
Poland, Austria and Turkey .	(Carlowitz). . .	1699
Russia and Turkey . . .	(Adrianople) .	1713
Great Britain, France, Spain,	(Utrecht) . .	1713
States General, Portugal		
and the Two Sicilies		

The Emperor and Turkey	(Passarowitz)	.	1718
Russia and Sweden .	(Nystadt) .	.	1721
The Emperor and Spain	(Vienna) .	.	1725
The Emperor and Russia	(Vienna) .	.	1726
The Emperor and the King of Prussia	(Wusterhausen)	.	1726
Great Britain, the States General and the Emperor	(Vienna) .	.	1731
Russia, Denmark and the Emperor	(Copenhagen)	.	1732
France and the Emperor .	(Vienna) .	.	1738
The Emperor, Sweden, Russia and Turkey	(Belgrade) .	.	1739
France and Turkey .	(Capitulations)	.	1740
Great Britain, France and the States General	(Aix-la-Chapelle)	.	1748
The Empress and Prussia .	(Hubertsburg)	.	1763
Great Britain, France and Spain	(Paris) . .	.	1763
Russia and Poland .	. .	.	1768
Russia, Prussia and Austria .	(First Partition Treaty)		1772
Russia and Turkey .	(Kainardji) . .		1774
France and the United States	(Friendship and Commerce)		1778
The Emperor and Prussia .	(Teschen) .	.	1779
Russia, Sweden and Denmark	(First Armed Neutrality)		1780
Great Britain, France, Spain and the United States	(Versailles) .	.	1783
Great Britain and France .	(Commerce) .	.	1786
United States and France .	. .	.	1788
The Emperor and Turkey .	(Szistowe) .	.	1791
Russia, Prussia and Austria .	(Second Partition Treaty)		1793
Russia, Prussia and Austria .	(Third Partition Treaty)		1795
United States and Spain .	(Commerce and Boundary of Mexico)		1795

The Emperor and France . . (Campo Formio) .	1797
United States and Prussia . (Commerce) . .	1799
United States and France . (Commerce) . .	1800
Russia, Sweden, Denmark and Prussia	(Second Armed Neutrality)	1800
Great Britain, France, Spain and the Netherlands	(Amiens) . .	1802
The Emperor and France . (Presburg) . .	1805
France and Prussia . . (Tilsit) . .	1807
Great Britain and Turkey . (Constantinople) .	1809
Russia and Turkey . . (Bucharest) . .	1812
Great Britain, Austria, Prussia, Russia and France . .	(First Peace of Paris)	May 30, 1814
Great Powers and the Netherlands	(Convention, Paris)	July 11, 1814
Great Britain and United States	(Ghent) . .	1814
Great Britain, Prussia, Russia, Austria, Spain, Sweden, Portugal and France	(Congress of Vienna, Final Act) .	June 9, 1815
Great Britain, Austria, Russia, Prussia and France	(Second Peace of Paris)	Nov. 5, 1815
Great Powers and Switzerland	(Paris) . . .	Nov. 20, 1815
Great Britain and United States	(Fisheries and Boundaries)	1818
United States and Central America	(Commerce) . .	1825
Russia and Turkey . . (Ackerman) . .	1826
United States and Brazil . (Commerce) . .	1828
Russia and Turkey . . (Adrianople) .	1829
Great Powers and Belgium . (London) . .	1831
United States and Mexico . (Commerce) . .	1831
Great Britain, France, Russia and Bavaria	(London) . .	1832
United States and Chili . (Commerce) . .	1832
Russia and Turkey . . (Unkiar Skelessi) .	1833
Russia and Turkey . . (St. Petersburg) .	1834
United States and Spain . (Commerce) . .	1834
United States and Peru . (Commerce) . .	1836
United States and Ecuador . (Commerce) . .	1839

Great Britain, France, Russia . . . . . July 18,			
and Denmark			1863
Five Great Powers . . . . . Nov. 14,			
			1863
Geneva . . . . (Convention) . 1864			
Austria and Prussia . . (Prague) . . 1866			
United States and Russia . (Cession of Alaska) 1867			
The Six Powers, the Netherlands (London) . . 1867			
and Belgium			
Geneva . . . . (Convention) . . 1868			
St. Petersburg . . . (Declaration of) . 1868			
Great Britain and the North 1870			
German Confederation			
Great Britain and France 1870			
S. German States and North (Versailles, German Jan. 18,			
German Confederation Empire formed) 1871			
Great Britain, France, Turkey (Conference and Jan.			
and Russia Treaty of London) 1871			
France and Germany . . (Versailles) . . Feb. 26,			
			1871
France and Germany . . (Frankfort) . . May,			
			1871
Great Britain and the United (Washington Arbi- May,			
States tration, Alabama, 1871			
San Juan and			
Fisheries)			
Russia and Turkey . . (San Stefano) . . 1878			
Great Britain, Russia, France, (Congress and . 1878			
Austria-Hungary, Italy, Ger- Treaty of Berlin)			
many and Turkey			
Great Britain and Turkey . (Convention) . 1878			
Prussia and Austria 1879			
United States and Mexico . (Boundary) . . 1884			
Great Britain, France, Germany, (Berlin Act) . 1885			
Portugal, and Belgium			
Great Britain and many Powers (Brussels Act) . 1890			
Great Britain and Germany . (Africa) . . 1890			
Great Britain and France . (Zanzibar) . . 1890			
China and Japan . . . (Shimonoseki) . 1895			

Great Britain and United (Venezuela) . . 1897
States
United States and Spain . . (Paris) . . 1898
Hague . . . . . (Conference) . . 1899
United States and Spain . (Treaty of Peace and 1902
Amity)
United States and Cuba 1903
Great Britain, many Powers (Submission to 1903
and Venezuela   Hague Tribunal)
Great Britain, France and (Morocco) . . 1904
Spain
Great Britain and France . (Siam) . . . 1904
Great Britain and Japan . (Alliance) . . 1905
Japan and Russia . . (Portsmouth, U.S.A.) 1905
Six Great Powers, Belgium, (Morocco) . . 1906
The Netherlands, Spain,
Portugal, Sweden, the
United States, and Morocco
Geneva . . . . (Convention) . 1906
Hague . . . . . (Conference) . . 1907
Great Britain and the United (*Modus Vivendi*) . 1907
States
Great Britain and Russia . (Persia) . . 1907
Great Britain and the United (Fishery Arbitra- . 1909
States   tion)
London . . . . (Conference and 1909
Declaration of)
Balkan League and Turkey . . . . . May 30,
1913
Greece, Serbia, Roumania and (Bucharest) . . Aug. 6,
Bulgaria   1913
Greece and Serbia . . (Defensive Alliance) 1913

INDEX

14

Printed by Hazell, Watson & Viney, Ld., London and Aylesbury, England.

www.ingramcontent.com/pod-product-compliance
Lightning Source LLC
Chambersburg PA
CBHW021542260326
41914CB00001B/127